The Authorities

Powerful Wisdom from Leaders in the Field

BRIAN KLODT

Real Estate Investor and founder of the 100 Goals Club

AuthoritiesPress

Publisher
Authorities Press
Markham, ON
Canada

Printed in the United States and Canada.

This book is written for people, of all ages, looking to achieve more in life through real estate investing.

I dedicate this book to my wife, Kathy, and my children, Karah and Maddie, the most important people in my life, and who have contributed greatly to the writing of this book and living out this strategy.

FOREWORD

Experts are to be admired for their knowledge, but they often remain unrecognized by the general public because they save their information and insights for paying customers and clients. There are many experts in a given field, but their impact is limited to the handful of people with whom they work.

Unlike experts, authorities share their knowledge and expertise far more broadly, so they make a big impact on the world. Authorities become known and admired as leading experts and, as such, typically do very well economically and professionally. Most authorities are also mature enough to know that part of the joy of monetary success is the accompanying moral and spiritual obligation to give back.

Many people want to learn and work with well-respected and generous authorities, but don't always know where to find them. They may be known to their peers, or within a specific community, but have not had the opportunity to reach a wider audience. At one time, they might have submitted a proposal to the For Dummies or Chicken Soup for the Soul series of books, but it's now almost impossible to get accepted as a new author in such branded book series.

It is more than fitting that Raymond Aaron, an internationally known and respected authority in his own right, would be the one to recognize the need for a new venue in which authorities could share their considerable knowledge with readers everywhere. As the only author ever to be included in both of the book series mentioned above, Raymond has had the opportunity to give back and he understands how crucial it is for authorities to have a platform from which to share their expertise.

TABLE OF CONTENTS

ACKNOWLEDGEMENTS

Thank you to my wife, **Kathy**, who has been a wonderful partner and wife for the past 25 + years as we developed our real estate investments into a key part of our life adventure.

Thank you to my parents **Morley** and **Gunnell** for being supportive every step of the way.

Thank you to my Karate Sensei, who was influential during my twenties and got me thinking about real estate investing in the first place.

Thank you to **Dr. Christopher Cooper** and **Jamie Stowe** for their magnificent work done to restore our Gables on the Park properties. They are true craftsmen, and people devoted to the preservation of heritage properties.

Thank you to **Tom** and **Nick Karadza**, of Rock Star Real Estate, for providing such an inspirational investment club for real estate investors and those interested in entrepreneurial training and personal development, to "Live Life on Your Terms", inspiring me greatly over the last decade. To our Rock Star coach, **Mike Desormeaux**, for helping guide our most recent real estate transactions.

And finally, thank you to **Raymond Aaron** for this wonderful opportunity to publish my book through his Authorities program, and provide meaningful mentorship through his Monthly Mentor® program.

INTRODUCTION

This book introduces you to *The Authorities* — individuals who have distinguished themselves in life and in business. Authorities make a big impact on the world. Authorities are leaders in their chosen fields. Authorities typically do very well financially, and are evolved enough to know that part of the joy of monetary success is the accompanying social, moral and spiritual obligation to give back.

Authorities are not just outstanding. They are also *known* to be outstanding.

This additional element begins to explain the difference between two strategic business and life concepts — one that seems great, but isn't, and the other that fills in the essential missing gap of the first.

The first concept is "the expert."

What is an expert? The real definition is …

EXPERT: *a person who knows stuff*

People who have attained a very senior academic degree (like a PhD or an MD) definitely know stuff. People who read voraciously and retain what they read definitely know stuff. Unfortunately, just because you know stuff does not mean that anyone respects the fact that you do. Even though some experts are successful, alas, most are not — because knowing stuff is not enough.

Well, then, what is the missing piece?

What the expert lacks, "the authority" has. The authority both knows stuff and is *known* to know stuff. So, more simply …

AUTHORITY: *a person who is known as an expert*

The difference is not subtle. The difference is not merely semantic. The difference is enormous.

When it comes to this subject, there are actually three categories in which people fall:

- People who don't know much and are unsuccessful in life and in business. Most people fall in this category.

- People who know stuff, but still don't leave much of a footprint in the world. There are a lot of people like this.

- Experts who are also *known* as experts become authorities and authorities are always wondrously successful. Authorities are able to contribute more to humanity through both their chosen work and their giving back.

This book is about the highest category, *The Authorities* — people who have reached the peak in their field and are known as such.

You will definitely know some of *The Authorities* in this book, many of whom are true pioneers, exceptional people who have inspired millions and who have deservedly gained their status as experts in their fields. Others are just as exceptional, although perhaps not as well known, and our aim is to introduce them and their inspirational work to you.

Our featured author, Brian Klodt, is a successful real estate investor who has dedicated his life to living a goal inspired life and helping others achieve their full potential. At the age of 30 he was inspired to write out 100 Life Goals, one of which led him and his wife Kathy to purchase all four homes on his street while developing a unique rental strategy with furnished home rentals. His strategy of buying "neighbour" houses on his own street or in his own neighbourhood has been the foundation for the financial success for him and his wife and paved the way to achieve many of their goals.

A passionate believer in self help and personal development, Brian is also the founder of the 100 Goals Club, an organization he is building to help people write down and achieve their life goals. Members will focus on such areas as Personal Development, Friends and Family, Health and Fitness, Hobbies and Passions, Finances, Career, Travel, Adventure, Lifestyle, Giving Back and Leaving a Legacy.

In his chapter about real estate investing, Brian invites you to look at your neighbours' houses in an entirely new way, which will have you watching for opportunities to purchase nearby homes and turn them in to a long-term asset that you can use as part of your retirement plan (to develop significant wealth), while enjoying all the benefits of owning property close by.

This chapter titled, *Buy Your Neighbour's House*, is for every person seeking to live a good life. Brian and his wife Kathy are proof that by investing in residential real estate you can become a millionaire and live the life you want.

Whether you are thinking about buying just one property or several, this chapter will inspire you to act and take advantage of purchase opportunities when the timing is right. Read this chapter, and commit to making real estate investing a key part of your financial strategy.

Read each chapter carefully to learn and to see the business potential that may be possible between yourself and each one of *The Authorities*. You may well be able to become their client or, possibly, do business with them in other ways.

They are *The Authorities*. Learn from them. Connect with them. Let them uplift you. Learning from them and working with them is the secret ingredient for success which may well allow you to rise to the level of Authority soon.

To be considered for inclusion in a subsequent edition of *The Authorities*, register to attend a future event at www.aaron.com/events where you will be interviewed and considered.

Buy Your Neighbour's House

The #1 Real Estate Strategy to Develop Wealth on Your Own Street

BRIAN KLODT

Get rich with the secret goldmine that lives next door!

Have you been searching for a way to improve your financial outlook? Are you worried about having enough money in your retirement years? Are you living the life you want? Do you know what would have the biggest impact on your financial future?

In this chapter, I explain why buying investment real estate, and specifically why buying your neighbour's house (or a house on your street or in your neighbourhood), is a desirable way to develop your wealth, support you in your quest to live a good life and help fund you in your retirement years. Your neighbour's "house" could also be a condominium, townhouse or another type of residential property. I will explain in detail the reasons for doing so along with helpful information on how to go about doing it. Real Estate is one of the best vehicles for the average family to develop long-term wealth and transform financial health.

MY STORY

My story begins in 1989 at the age of 28 years old when, at the peak of the Canadian real estate market, I purchased my first house. It was an existing duplex, a two and one-half story Victorian brick house in a low-income neighbourhood. I bought it for $150,000. Although hindsight is 20/20, looking back I purchased a house doing everything wrong. I bought a good house in a poor location and purchased it at the worst possible time. The conventional wisdom is that you should buy the worst house on the street in the best location. I did the exact opposite. The house came with an existing tenant in the second-floor apartment. The house also had a large unfinished basement. A friend built a basement apartment for me (with some of my limited experience help), and I then had a triplex. After living on the main floor for one year, my fiancé moved into the basement apartment, and we worked to complete the finishing touches there for one more year. In 1991 we were married, and we both moved from our respective apartments to the second-floor apartment, where we fixed up that unit and continued to live there for our first year of marriage. After the third year living in our triplex, we decided to move back to my hometown, about 20 minutes away. It was in an up and coming downtown neighbourhood on a picturesque street, just a few blocks up from Lake Ontario and two beautiful parks. We were able to keep our triplex, because of the good income coming from the three units, there was enough money to pay for all our expenses. It also provided an additional cash flow to put into the bank for all the improvements the house would need. I continued to manage many tenants over the 25 years we owned this house, selling in 2014 for $340,000.

In our second house in the neighbouring city, we began to raise our family in what was just a small 950 square-foot Victorian century home. Our children were born in 1994 and 1998. We had outgrown the house with the birth of our second child, but we loved the neighbourhood location so much we continued to live in the house. We hired an architect to design an addition for our home with the thought we would make the house bigger to live in, but in 2003 the house next door came up for sale. The house was very similar except that it had a large addition in the rear which resulted in a large three-bedroom house. Since we had been receiving income from the triplex for all those years it was a natural thought to purchase our neighbour's house and rent out the house we had been living in. The house was more than double the price we paid for our first house. We asked our friends and family to help us move all our possessions 30 feet south to the house next door, without the need to rent a truck or moving company. We loved transitioning into this larger house, which was in an even better location, being one home closer to the lake.

In 2005, the third of what was only four houses on our block came up for sale. Already owning two of the four houses on the same street, it was again natural for us to think about purchasing the third house. I had set a goal at age 30 to become a millionaire and real estate was becoming our main method for the achievement of this goal. In this case, the market was hot again, and we knew that we would need to act quickly. The night the house came up for sale, we approached the seller's real estate agent directly about purchasing the house. There was going to be another offer made on the property even though the house had just come up for sale. To ensure we were successful with our offer, we proposed $2,000 more than the asking price and became the proud owners of the third of four houses on our street. This house was being used by the prior owner as a hair salon and had been set up to be very eclectic in terms of paint colours (gold crown moulding, orange walls) and kitchen finishing. The kitchen cupboard doors actually had colourful gems and decorative colours affixed to them. We renovated this house and turned it into a rental unit.

In 2006, the owner of the remaining house on the street approached us and asked if we would be interested in purchasing their house should they ever decide to sell. Six months later, at Christmas time, they left a note on our door saying they wanted to talk to us. It turns out they had an opportunity to move out west and were looking to see if we wanted to buy their house. With a loan from my parents for the down payment, we were able to purchase the fourth house on the block. We now owned an entire street of four heritage century homes, all built in the late 1800's, three of them protected with heritage designation. It was difficult to decide whether to stay in our second house or move to this fourth house. The decision to move once again was made due to the larger lot, a wood burning fireplace in the living room, and granite counters in an updated kitchen. The trade-off was that the house was only about 1,200 square feet, smaller than the second house we had lived in. Regardless, we loved this new house. Our children had now lived in three consecutive houses all on the same street.

In 2017, our real estate story of owning all four houses on the street was featured in a real estate investment club's newsletter and we were honoured as members of the month. I was asked to speak at one of their member events on how we were able to accomplish this, and about the unique rental strategy we developed along the way, which you'll read about shortly.

WHY INVESTMENT REAL ESTATE?

Of all the investment classes, real estate is the foundation of a large percentage of high net worth individuals. Since there is only a limited supply of land, and the population of the world continues to increase at record pace, real estate will continue to increase in price when viewed as a long-term investment. There are several unique advantages to owning investment real estate:

- Real estate is something the average person can understand.

- You can invest in real estate while having a full-time career and treat it as your "side hustle" or hobby.

- You can rent out your real estate and have tenants pay off your debt.

- Over time, you can raise the price of your rent to improve your positive cash flow. Positive cash flow means that you'll have money left over after paying for all of the expenses associated with owning the property. When tenants change over, rents can be adjusted to the going market rate. Mortgage payment remains constant, depending on your mortgage term and prevailing interest rates.

- By buying property in "up and coming" neighbourhoods, you can multiply your equity and cash flow gains as the desirability of living in your neighbourhood increases. Equity is the part of the house that you own versus the part the bank owns. Equity is based on the current market value of the house minus the amount remaining on your mortgage.

- Through leverage, you gain the benefits, over time, of controlling a very large asset and the gains associated with it, with a much smaller down payment. As an example, you may only put a 10% down payment to purchase a house which is worth ten times more than your down payment. The gains you make, however, relate to the full value of the house purchase, not just your 10% down payment. As a very simple example using easy round numbers, let's say you put 10% down to purchase a $100,000 house, or $10,000. If your house appreciates 5% in one year, your $100,000 house will be worth $105,000. You've made a gain of $5,000 on your $10,000 investment ($105,000 minus $100,000), which represents a 50% gain ($5,000 gain / $10,000 down payment). This illustrates the remarkable concept and benefit of leverage.

- You can increase the value of your real estate through your own "sweat equity," in which you make your own improvements instead of paying someone else. Sweat equity is a term for using your own physical labour (where you just might get sweaty), resulting in an increase in the value or equity portion of your house because of the improvements. An example would be removing carpeting on your own and installing laminate or hardwood flooring in its place, increasing the value of your house by $10,000. However, you only spent $5,000 on the flooring and materials.

Some people strive to become millionaires to support their retirement goals. Investing in real estate for the long-term is a proven way to become a millionaire. As a continuation of our simple example, let's say you purchase a single-family house for $100,000 which produces a break-even cash flow. After having your tenants pay off your mortgage over 25 years, you'll own the house outright, but after 25 years, the house is likely to be worth at least double what you paid for it. At 5% appreciation per year (quite possible in some locations and markets), your $100,000 house will be worth more than $300,000. Depending on the actual home purchase price, it is possible your house will be worth more than $1,000,000. If your house doesn't appreciate significantly, that's okay too. You'll still have a substantially paid off asset when you're ready for retirement.

As discussed in "my story," in 1992 my wife Kathy and I purchased our first house in my hometown which we lived in for 11 years. We then purchased our neighbour's houses in 2003, 2005 and 2006. We did this while continuing to own and rent the triplex house we purchased in 1989. All of these subsequent house purchases have more than tripled in value since time of purchase. We have developed and been blessed with high net worth and cash flow as a result of investment in real estate, and it has allowed us to live our dream life. Net worth is the resulting value of all the things you own (your assets), minus the amount of money you owe. High net worth is the benefit of investing in real estate long-term. It can support you financially in many ways and, in particular, with achieving and living your lifestyle goals. In our case, it helped finance international travel to support our first daughter to compete around the world on the Canadian National Rhythmic Gymnastics Team. We were able to fund our second daughter's equestrian life, including more than ten years of lessons and competitions, leading up to her competing at one of the top equestrian events in Canada, The Royal Winter Fair. We've also enjoyed traveling to more than 20 countries including France, Japan and Spain. All of this is a result of having built up good positive cash flow and equity in buying our neighbours' houses. Buying just one of your neighbours' houses will set you up nicely to support your retirement years.

WHY BUY YOUR NEIGHBOUR'S HOUSE?

There are the obvious financial and lifestyle advantages to buying real estate as discussed above, but why, specifically, am I recommending you that buy your neighbour's house? How often have you driven by a house in your own neighbourhood and wondered to yourself "how much does that house cost?" Have you thought fleetingly, "I wonder if we could purchase that house?" Some of the reasons for buying and owning one (or more) of your neighbours' houses include:

1. It is easy to maintain your neighbour's house and meet with its tenants.

It takes much less time to service your properties, meet with tenants and handle maintenance issues when they are right next door. One of the disadvantages of owning real estate in other cities is that tenants have a track record of not showing up when they say they will. If that happens and your house is next door, there's no travel time lost, and it's not a big deal. Meeting a plumber who is doing work on your property is also more convenient. The time savings of managing property close by are significant.

2. You'll be motivated to keep them in good condition.

You won't forget to cut the grass or take care of maintenance issues as you will take pride in having the houses that are next to you look good. Unfortunately, that is not the case with some landlord owned properties in remote cities. You can often spot the landlord owned properties as the ones with uncut grass and houses with maintenance issues. When properties are well maintained and cared for, they'll be worth more money and rent for a higher dollar amount.

3. You have a natural screen against attracting "bad" tenants.

Selecting good tenants is important to your success as a landlord. Any "bad" tenant who is likely to cause you issues or not pay rent will likely not apply to live in your house, choosing instead to live somewhere else. It's too easy for a landlord who lives next door to know when the tenant is home and follow up directly for any payment or concerns, for example, partying or loud music. But if a "good" tenant likes you and the property, they'll see it as an advantage that their landlord lives close by, so that they can look after maintenance issues quicker. We have had a 15-year excellent track record of attracting good tenants in our "neighbour" houses.

4. Improvements to your house will add value to your house "next door."

Curb appeal matters and being able to control and enhance the streetscape of multiple properties side by side will increase their overall value. Curb appeal is the first impression someone has of your house, either positive or negative. When you own two, three or more homes on your own street, making "curb appeal" improvements is a benefit to all of them, in addition to making you feel good about how they look. Spending $5,000 in improvements on one of the houses could multiply the overall value to your streetscape by a two to three times multiplying factor.

Landscaping is a good example of an exterior improvement that improves curb appeal. This helps when you go to the bank for financing, and they send out a bank appraiser to appraise the value of your house(s), as the properties will appraise at a higher value. If you ever decide to sell one of your houses, the ability to ensure that they all are in top shape and look good from the street is in your total control. That is not always the case. Some people find when they go to sell a home, the house next door detracts from the streetscape and value of their home. Some of the things we've done to our homes over the years include:

- Upgraded our driveways from gravel to pavement with perimeter pavers

- Added interlocking pathways to the doorsteps

- Hired a landscape architect to design a circular garden with perennials and a landscape planter

- Installed heritage house number signs

- Contracted front porch restorations to remedy the impacts of age and weather

- Hired an architect and professional carpenter to design and build two heritage swing entry gates leading from the front to the rear of each property

- Updated porch / exterior lighting fixtures

With these types of exterior improvements to your homes, you will improve the overall value of your homes dramatically and feel good about doing so. Nobody will call you a "slumlord" when you own beautifully cared for homes with curb appeal.

5. They're easier to rent for a higher price as a "furnished rental."

Most home rentals are rented as unfurnished houses on a one-year lease. With your house being just next door, operating your homes as furnished rentals can be done by yourself easily, improving your positive cash flow. Think Airbnb, Vacation Rentals by Owner (VRBO) or short-term rentals on KIJIJI. As a furnished rental, tenants will pay a higher premium for rent as you will be providing the house with furniture, bedding and other accessories.

This provides a financial "up-side" to your rental revenue which could boost your positive cash flow by more than 50%. This could also make the difference as to whether or not your property will produce a positive cash flow. With a furnished rental, you'll be allowing tenants to move in with just a suitcase as if they were checking into a hotel. The types of people looking for furnished rentals include:

- Corporate executives or professionals

- Homeowners during major renovations

- Homeowners dealing with insurance claim disasters (i.e. house fire, flooding)

- Marital breakups. This is a big source for our tenants, who often need a place for an "open-ended" period of time while they figure out next steps, often up to one year, or more.

- People and families in transition. Often a couple or family will want to live in an area for a while before they decide if the area is the place they want to establish roots and purchase a house.

Our experience is that you can furnish an entire house for less than $10,000 and achieve payback within 18 months. The type of furnishings and services you'll need to provide will include kitchen utensils and accessories, beds and bedding, towels and linens, furniture, HDTV, artwork / décor, wireless internet, heat and hydro. You can hire a cleaner to perform a professional and thorough clean between tenants, or you can do this yourself.

6. You'll always know how your investment is performing.

You have a full view of your investment and can keep an eye on each house just by looking down (or up) the street. When you own traditional investments like stocks or mutual funds, you may not look at their performance or follow them closely enough to know how they are doing. You also have no control over how the company is managed or is performing. When you own property on the same street, you can't help but know how your houses are doing. If there's a problem with the roof and you notice shingles on the driveway after a windstorm, you can act on it right away before the roof leaks.

7. You can paint the houses your own colour scheme, increasing their market value.

You have total control over any paintable surfaces on your houses such as siding and door colours. Have someone you know or hire someone who is good with colours to help pick your colour scheme. This too helps with improving the "curb appeal." We painted all four of our houses a colour scheme based on an affirmation I learned while attending a seminar hosted by my karate sensei in the late 1980's. The affirmation "I am Happy, Healthy, Wealthy and Wise" has been a central and major influence in my life. I felt so strongly about this affirmation that more than 20 years ago I developed a system for filing my goals into these categories and gave each category a colour: the colour Blue for "Happy"—Blue Sky, Blue Water, Calmness; The colour Red for Healthy"—Red Blood, Red Tomatoes, Red Apples; The colour Green for "Wealthy"—Money and Wealth; and the colour Grey for "Wise"—Wise elders (and their grey hair). My wife and I chose to have our four Gables On The Park homes painted these four colours as part of our streetscaping and restoration improvement plan. For before and after photos, visit www.GablesOnThePark.com. The reason these unique colour choices work is that our homes are Victorian-era homes with intricate gingerbread and gables, which are known to be painted special colours during a restoration process. We were inspired by the famous San Francisco "Painted Ladies" homes, which are some of the most photographed houses in the world. But the bottom line is that when you own your own street someday, you too can choose your own colour scheme and improve their curb appeal. Please take a photo and send me the before and after photos!

HOW TO BUY YOUR NEIGHBOUR'S HOUSE.

The steps to follow in buying your neighbours house are:

1. Determine if buying your neighbour's house makes financial sense.

Since your neighbour's house is likely to be similar to your house, you can roughly figure out the carrying costs by basing the calculation on your current expenses and adjusting for the current market. Based on the estimated market value of the house, you can figure out what it would cost for another mortgage. Add to that the costs for property taxes and any other carrying costs, noting that in most rentals the tenants will pay the utility costs, including heat and hydro. Then research or ask around for what tenants in your area are paying per month to rent a house. Get some help online or from a realtor friend if you are not sure how to make this calculation. If the rent you can charge is higher than the expenses you will pay, the decision to buy your neighbour's house makes financial sense.

If the numbers don't add up keep in mind that it may be possible or necessary to renovate your neighbour's house to maximize your monthly income by adding a second suite such as a basement apartment. Sometimes this is required to make the property "cash flow" and is worth the time and effort to do so. Also consider the furnished rental option described above, which is another method to increase the rent amount.

2. Approach your neighbours to let them know you might be interested

if they were ever to sell.

Casually find out which of your neighbours are likely to be moving on within the next few years. For some, it could be highly unlikely, and for others, it could be sooner than you think. Depending on your relationship with your neighbours, you could even mention that you've read this book and are just curious about your long-term options. The other strategy is to just wait for a house on your street to get listed by a realtor. At that point, you can decide to pursue this strategy aggressively.

3. Get pre-qualified by your bank.

A key concept is that once you have developed equity in your primary residence, your bank will allow you to borrow against that equity to fund the down payment of your first investment property. It is possible that you can finance your entire down payment without coming up with additional money from other sources, based on the equity you hold in your primary residence. Approach your bank and ask them the question. They can do a rough calculation for you based on the approximate market value of your current house.

4. Choose a realtor to help you transact the purchase.

Since purchasing a house is such an important and significant financial transaction, you should seek the services of a qualified realtor to help you with the transaction. In our case, we purchased two of our three neighbours' homes without using a realtor, and one using the seller's realtor. But if we were to do this again, I would seriously consider hiring a realtor representing us as the buyer. We missed doing a home inspection on the purchase of one of our homes that a realtor would have recommended we do. A realtor will also take the pressure off of negotiating the best purchase price possible and completing all the paperwork correctly.

5. Be ready to buy when the opportunity presents itself.

With this real estate strategy, the key is to understand that when the opportunity presents itself, you have to be ready to act. Discuss with your partner and create a general agreement that you want to follow this strategy. When the third house on our street came up for sale, we had no forewarning, and we purchased the house the very night the for-sale sign went up. You may need to have patience as this strategy may take years to unfold, as it did in our case.

BUT WHAT IF YOU HAVEN'T PURCHASED YOUR FIRST HOUSE YET?

Don't worry if you have yet to purchase your first house as your primary residence. You have the added benefit of finding a neighbourhood where, once the time is right, this strategy could work. Look for neighbourhoods with homes that would provide you with a positive cash flow (the rental income will exceed the cost of your expenses, e.g. (mortgage, taxes etc.). Generally, this applies to starter homes. Buy in an up and coming location. Your investment will be improved dramatically if you can find a good location that is on its way up in value due to good demographics (people statistics), such as the number of people moving into your neighbourhood, their average income levels, etc. These are influenced by things that are happening in your neighbourhood to make it a more desirable place to live, such as improvements to the transportation system, urbanization and close proximity to water or a natural feature.

The strategy of buying your neighbour's house won't work in all situations. It won't work in high priced neighbourhoods where it's impossible to produce a positive cash flow (when your rental income is less than what you spend to own the property). It also won't work in locations where it's hard to rent. But don't worry. Most people have access to great investment properties within a one-to-two-hour radius of where they live. The key is to buy investment real estate, but start by looking on your own street and then in your own neighbourhood.

THE BIG PAYOFF

After paying off the mortgage for 25 years (the typical mortgage period on a house), you'll retire your debt with the bank and own the house outright. This will help you tremendously in your retirement years as now the money you were paying to the bank for your mortgage will become extra positive cash flow that will help you out in retirement years. Because your house was purchased next door or on your street, you'll have no problems continuing to rent out the house with minimal effort, as you've been doing for the past 25 years. It's like you developed a "money tree" in your own neighbourhood which keeps on giving. The house will also be worth hundreds of thousands of dollars. You could also consider selling and living off the proceeds from the sale of your house(s). You could downsize and live elsewhere, perhaps in a smaller and more affordable house in order to live off of all the equity you accumulated over the years of being a real estate investor on your own street.

It's also possible that you'll be approached by a developer to sell your homes if you happen to have purchased the house(s) next door. If you own land in a municipality where your zoning permits higher density housing, this could turn out to be a highly profitable strategy. And if you are entrepreneurial and want to be your own developer, you could develop the site yourself. It could be worth the time, effort and risk if you are up for it. In our own city, there are numerous sites where developers have been purchasing adjacent homes and businesses with the goal of getting approval to tear them down and build something grander.

The equity you gain from owning real estate will give you a huge advantage to help you do other amazing things. This principle alone has supported our family well over the past 25 years and allowed us to purchase our additional properties which led to us owning our street. It has also given us the financial resources to support our children with their extracurriculars, and family travel, as our net worth has grown.

WHAT DOES IT TAKE TO DO THIS?

Developing wealth as an active real estate investor does require you to have good ambition. It involves a willingness to take on some risk. It helps if you can develop some handyman skills or find someone you trust to do that for you. It takes an attitude to treats tenants like you'd like to be treated yourself. When issues come up dealing with tenants or maintenance, you'll need to focus on why you're doing this and the long-term benefits.

Owning physical real estate isn't for everyone. You need to have a certain temperament to deal with the tenants and maintenance issues or trust others to look after these things for you. For those who can never see themselves as landlords, there are other ways to benefit in real estate. For example, as a silent partner in a joint venture agreement or investor in a real estate investment trust (REIT). REIT's were established for small investors who were not interested in the responsibilities of property maintenance or managing tenants directly. REIT's are intended for people who want to be able to invest in real estate without the large capital required to purchase real estate directly.

Being goal driven was one of the reasons that led my wife Kathy and I to be successful not only with real estate but in other areas of life. In my book, 100 Life Goals, I write about 100 goals that will transform your life and give you the confidence to make the kind of decisions that will lead to success in real estate and other areas.

WHAT NEXT?

After following the advice on the "how to" section above, you could join a local real estate club to see other real estate investors in action and learn from them. I'm fortunate to be a member of a local real estate investment club, Rock Star Real Estate, that is helping hundreds of real estate investors achieve financial independence, with their slogan "Your Life, Your Terms." Once they heard of our story and strategy, they asked me to present to their members at one of their events on "Owning an Entire Street: How to go from one property to Owning the Whole Street." They also helped our daughter purchase her first investment property, a century duplex townhouse.

While it's rather intuitive that owning properties close to home makes the most sense, owning investment properties on the same street is not something that happens too often and is likely not something that would be discussed at a local real estate club. My hope is that in reading about this strategy, you develop the awareness that if one of your neighbours' houses comes up for sale, you take a serious look at whether this strategy could work for you. If you do, I'd love to hear about your story someday. Contact me through www.100GoalsClub.com.

Branding Small Business

RAYMOND AARON

Branding is an incredibly important tool for creating and building your business. Large companies have been benefiting from branding ever since people first started selling things to other people. Branding made those businesses big.

If you're a small business owner, you probably imagine that small companies are different and don't need branding as much as large companies do. Not true. The truth is small businesses need branding just as much, if not more, than large companies.

Perhaps you've thought about branding, but assumed you'd need millions of dollars to do it properly, or that branding is just the same thing as marketing. Nothing could be further from the truth.

Marketing is the engine of your company's success. Branding is the fuel in that engine.

In the old days, salespeople were a big part of the selling process. They recommended one product over another and laid out the reasons why it was better. Salespeople had credibility because they knew about all the products, and customers often took the advice they had to offer.

Today, consumers control the buying process. They shop in big box stores, super-sized supermarkets, and over the Internet — where there are no salespeople. Buyers now get online and gather information beforehand. They learn about all the products available and look to see if there really is any difference between them. Consumers also read reviews and check social media to see if both the company and the product are reputable. In other words, they want to know what the brand is all about.

The way of commerce used to be: "Nothing happens till something is sold." Today it's: "Nothing happens till something is branded!"

DEFINING A BRAND

A brand is a proper name that stands for something. It lives in the consumer's mind, has positive or negative characteristics, and invokes a feeling or an image. In short, it's a person's perception of a product or a company.

When all goes well, consumers associate the same characteristics with a brand that the company talks about in its advertising, public relations, marketing and sales materials. Of course, when a product doesn't live up to what the company says about it, the brand gets a bad reputation. On the other hand, if a product or service over-delivers on the promises made, the brand can become a superstar.

RECOGNIZING BRANDING AND ITS CHARACTERISTICS

Branding is the science and art of making something that isn't unique, unique. Branding in the marketplace is the same as branding on a ranch. On a ranch, ranchers use branding to differentiate their cattle from every other rancher's cattle (because all cattle look pretty much the same). In the marketplace, branding is what makes a product stand out in a crowd of similar products. The right branding gets you noticed, remembered and sold — or perhaps I should say bought, because today it is all about buying, not selling.

There are four main characteristics of branding that make it an integral part of the marketing and purchasing process.

1. Branding makes you trustworthy and known

Branding makes a product more special than other products. With branding, a normal, everyday product has a personality, and a first and last name, and people know who you are.

In today's marketplace, most products are, more or less, just like their competition. Toilet paper is toilet paper, milk is milk, and a grocery store by any other name is still a grocery store. However, branding takes a product and makes it unique. For example, high-quality drinking water is available from just about every tap in the Western world and it's free, but people pay good money for it when it comes in a bottle. Branding takes bottled water and makes Evian.

Furthermore, every aspect of your brand gives potential customers a feeling or comfort level that they associate with you. The more powerful and positive that feeling is, the more easily and more frequently they will want to do business with you and, indeed, will do business with you.

2. Branding differentiates you from others

Strong branding makes you better than your competition, and makes your product name memorable and easy to remember. Even if your product is absolutely the same as every other product like it, branding makes it special. Branding makes it the first product a consumer thinks about when deciding to make a purchase.

Branding also makes a product seem popular. Everyone knows about it, which implicitly says people like it. And, if people like it, it must be good.

3. Branding makes you worth more money

The stronger your branding is, the more likely people are willing to spend that little bit extra because they believe you, your product, your service, or your business are worth it. They may say they won't, but they will. They do it all the time.

For example, a one-pound box of Godiva chocolates costs about $40; the same weight of Hershey's Kisses costs about $4. The quality of the chocolate isn't ten times greater. The reason people buy Godiva is that the brand Godiva means "gift" whereas the brand Hershey means "snack". Gifts obviously cost more than snacks.

4. Branding pre-sells your product

In the buying age, people most often make the decision on which products to pick up before they walk into the store. The stronger the branding, the more likely people are to think in terms of your product rather than the product category. For example, people are as likely, maybe even more likely, to add Hellmann's to the shopping list as they are to write down simply mayo. The same is true for soda, ketchup, and many other products with successful, strong branding.

Plus, as soon as a shopper gets to the shelf, branding can provide a quick reminder of what products to grab in a few ways:

- An icon or logo
- A specific color
- An audio icon

BRANDING IN A SMALL BUSINESS

Big companies spend millions of dollars on advertising, marketing, and public relations (PR) to build recognition of a new product name. They get their selling messages out to the public using television, radio, magazines, and the Internet. They can even throw money at damage control when necessary. The strategies for branding are the same in a small business, but the scale, costs, and a few of the tactics change.

Make your brand name work harder

The name of a small business can mean everything in terms of branding. Your brand name needs to work harder for your business than you do. It's the first thing a prospective customer sees, and it is how they will remember you. A brand name has to be memorable when spoken, and focused in its meaning. If the name doesn't represent what consumers believe about a product and the company that makes it, then that brand will fail.

In building your product's reputation and image, less is often significantly more. Make sure the name you choose immediately gives a sense of what you do.

Large corporations have millions of dollars to take a meaningless brand name and make it stand for something. Small businesses don't, so use words that really mean something. Strive for something interesting and be right on point. You don't need to be boring.

Plumbers, for example, would do well setting themselves apart with names like "The On-Time Plumber" or "24/7 Plumbing". The same is true for electricians, IT providers, or even marketing consultants. Plenty of other types of business are so general in nature they just don't work hard enough in a business or product name.

Even the playing field: The Net

The Internet has leveled the playing field for small businesses like nothing else. You can use the Internet in several ways to market your brand:

Website: Developing and maintaining a website is easier than ever. Anyone can find your business regardless of its size.

Social Media: Facebook and Twitter can promote your brand in a cost-effective manner.

BUILDING YOUR BRAND WITH THE BRANDING LADDER

Even if you do everything perfectly the first time (and I don't know anyone who does), branding takes time. How much time isn't just up to you, but you can speed things along by understanding the different levels of branding, as well as the business and marketing strategies that can get you to the top.

Introducing the Branding Ladder

Moving through the levels of branding is like climbing a ladder to the top of the marketplace. The Branding Ladder has five distinct rungs and, unlike stairs, you can't take them two at a time. You have to take them in order, and some businesses spend more time on each rung than others.

You can also think of the Branding Ladder in terms of a scale from zero to ten. Everyone starts at zero. If you properly climb the ladder, you can end up at 12 out of 10. The Branding Ladder below shows a special rung at the top of the ladder that can take your business over the top. The following section explains the Branding Ladder and how your small business can move up it.

THE BRANDING LADDER	
Brand Advocacy	12/10
Brand Insistence	10/10
Brand Preference	3/10
Brand Awareness	1/10
Brand Absence	0/10

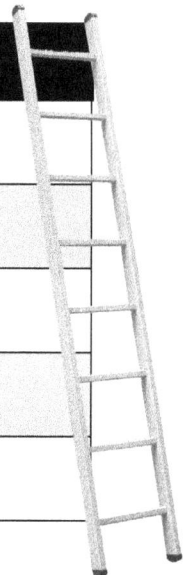

Rung 1: Living in the void

Your business, in fact every business, starts at the bottom rung, which is called brand absence, meaning you have no brand whatsoever except your own name. On a scale of one to ten, brand absence is, of course, zero. That's the worst place to live and obviously the most difficult entrepreneurially. The good news is that the only way is up.

Ninety-seven percent of businesses live on this rung of the Branding Ladder. They earn far less than they want to earn, far less than they should earn, and far less than they would earn if they did exactly the same work under a real brand.

Rung 2: Achieving awareness

Brand awareness is a good first step up the ladder to the second rung. Actually, it's really good, especially because 97 percent of businesses never get there. You want people to be aware of you. When person A speaks to person B and says, "Have you heard of "The 24/7 Plumber?" You want the answer to be "yes".

On that scale of one to ten, however, brand awareness is only a one. It's better than nothing, but not that much better. Although people know of your brand, being aware doesn't mean that they are interested in buying it. Coca Cola drinkers know about Pepsi, but they don't drink it.

Rung 3: Becoming the preferred brand

Getting to the third rung, brand preference, is definitely a real step up. This rung means that people prefer to use your product or service rather than that of your competition. They believe there is a real difference between you and others, and you're their first choice. This rung is a crucial branding stage for parity products, such as bottled water and breakfast cereals, not to mention plumbers, electricians, lawyers, and all the others. Brand preference is clearly better than brand awareness, but it's less than halfway up the ladder.

Car rental companies represent a perfect example of why brand preference may not be enough. When someone lands at an airport and needs to rent a car on the spot, he or she may go straight to the preferred rental counter. If that company has a car available, it's a sale. However, if all the cars for that company have been rented, the person will move to the next rental kiosk without much thought, because one rental car is just as good as another.

Exerting Brand Preference needs to be easy and convenient

If all you have is brand preference, your business is on shaky ground and you can lose business for the feeblest of reasons. Very few people go to a second or third supermarket just to find their favorite brand of bottled water. Similarly, a shopper may prefer one store over another but, if both stores sell the same products, he or she will often go to the closest store even if it is not the better liked one. The reason for staying nearby does not need to be a dramatic one — the shopper may simply be tired, on a tight schedule, or not in the mood to travel.

Rung 4: Making it you and only you

When your customers are so committed to your product or service that they won't accept a substitute, you have reached the fourth rung of the Branding Ladder. All companies strive to reach this place, called brand insistence.

Brand insistence means that someone's experience with a product in terms of performance, durability, customer service, and image has been sufficiently exceptional. As a result, the product has earned an incredible level of loyalty.

If the product isn't available where the customer is, he or she will literally not buy something else. Rather, the person will look for the preferred product elsewhere. Can you imagine what a fabulous place this is for a company to be? Brand insistence is the best of the best, the perfect ten out of ten, the whole ball of wax.

Apple is a perfect example of brand insistence

Apple users don't just think, they know in their heads and hearts, that anything made by Apple is technologically-advanced, user-friendly, and just all-around superior. Committed to everything Apple, Mac users won't even entertain the thought that a PC may have positive attributes.

Apple people love everything about their Macs, iPads, iPhones, the Mac stores and all those apps. When the company introduces a new product, many of its brand-insistent fans actually wait in line overnight to be one of the first to have it. Steve Jobs is one of their idols.

Considering one big potential problem

Unfortunately, you can lose brand insistence much more quickly than you can achieve it. Brand-insistent customers have such high expectations that they can be disillusioned or disappointed by just one bad product experience. You also have to consistently reinforce the positives because insistence can fade over time. Even someone who has bought and re-bought a specific brand of car for the last 20 years can decide it's just time for a change. That's how fickle the world is.

At ten out of ten, brand insistence may seem like the top rung of the ladder, but it's not. One rung is actually better, and it involves getting your brand-insistent customers to keep polishing your brand for you.

Rung 5: Getting customers to do the work for you

Brand advocacy is the highest rung on the ladder. It's better than ten out of ten because you have customers who are so happy with your product that they want everyone to know about it and use it. Think of them as uber-fans. Not only do they recommend you to friends and family, they also practically shout your praises from the rooftops, interrupt conversations among strangers to give their opinion, and tell everyone they meet how fantastic you are. Most companies can only aspire to this level of customer satisfaction. Apple is one of the few large corporations in recent history that has brand advocates all over the world.

- Brand advocacy does the following five extraordinary things for your company. Brand advocacy:

- Provides a level of visibility that you couldn't pay for if you tried. Brand advocates are so enthusiastic they talk about you all the time, and reach people in ways general media and public relations can't. You get great visibility because they make sure people actually listen.

- Delivers free advertising and public relations. Companies love the extra super-positive messaging, all for free.

- Affords a level of credibility that literally can't be bought. Brand advocates are more than just walking testimonials. They are living proof that you are the best.

- Provides pre-sold prospective customers. Advocate recommendations carry so much weight that they are worth much more than plain referrals. They deliver customers ready and committed to purchasing your product or service.

- Increases profits exponentially. Brand advocates are money-making machines for your business because they increase sales and decrease marketing costs.

For these reasons, brand advocacy is 12 out of 10!!

BRANDING YOURSELF: HOW TO DO SO IN FOUR EASY WAYS

If you're interested in branding your product or company, you may not be sure where to begin. The good news: I'm here to help. You can brand in many ways, but here I pare it down to four ways to help you start:

Branding by association

This way involves hanging out with and being seen with people who are very much higher than you in your particular niche.

Branding by achievement

This way repurposes your previous achievements.

Branding by testimonial

This way makes use of the testimonials that you receive but have likely never used.

Branding by WOW

A WOW is the pleasantly unexpected, the equivalent of going the extra mile. The easiest and most certain way to WOW people is to tell them that you've written a book. To discover how you can write a book of own, go to www.BrandingSmallBusinessForDummies.com.

Happiness: How to Experience the "Real Deals"

MARCI SHIMOFF

I was 41 years old, stretched out on a lounge chair by my pool and reflecting on my life. I had achieved all that I thought I needed to be happy.

You see, when I was a child, I thought there would be five main things that would ensure that I'd be happy: a successful career helping people, a loving husband, a comfortable home, a great body, and a wonderful circle of friends. After years of study, hard work, and a few "lucky breaks," I finally had them all. (Okay, so my body didn't quite look like Halle Berry's—but four out of five isn't bad!) You think I'd have been on the top of the world.

But surprisingly I wasn't. I felt an emptiness inside that the outer successes of life couldn't fill. I was also afraid that if I lost any of those things, I might be miserable. Sadly, I knew I wasn't alone in feeling this way.

While happiness is the one thing we all truly want, so few people really experience the deep and lasting fulfillment that fills our soul. Why aren't we finding it?

Because, in the words of the old country western song, we're looking for happiness in "all the wrong places."

Looking around, I saw that the happiest people I knew weren't the most successful and famous. Some were married, some were single. Some had lots of money, and some didn't have a dime. Some of them even had health challenges. From where I stood, there seemed to be no rhyme or reason to what made people happy. The obvious question became: *Could a person actually be happy for no reason?*

I had to find out.

So I threw myself into the study of happiness. I interviewed scores of scientists, as well as 100 unconditionally happy people. (I call them the Happy 100.) I delved into the research from the burgeoning field of positive psychology, the study of the positive traits that enable people to enjoy meaningful, fulfilling, and happy lives.

What I found changed my life. To share this knowledge with others, I wrote a book called *Happy for No Reason: 7 Steps to Being Happy from the Inside Out*.

One day, as I sat down to compile my findings, all the pieces of the puzzle fell into place. I had a simple, but profound "a-ha"—there's a continuum of happiness:

Unhappy	Happy for Bad Reason	Happy for Good Reason	Happy for No Reason
↕	↕	↕	↕
Depressed	High from unhealthy addictions	Satisfaction from healthy experiences	Inner state of peace & well-being

EXTERNAL   INTERNAL

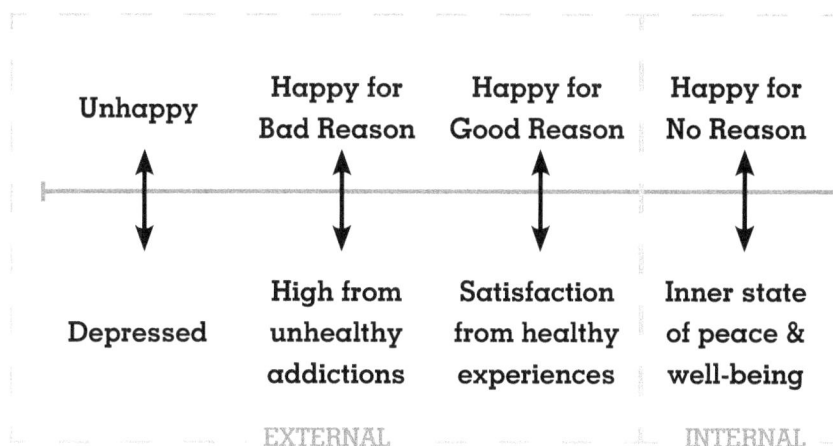

Unhappy: We all know what this means: life seems flat. Some of the signs are anxiety, fatigue, feeling blue or low—your "garden-variety" unhappiness. This isn't the same as clinical depression, which is characterized by deep despair and hopelessness that dramatically interferes with your ability to live a normal life, and for which professional help is absolutely necessary.

Happy for Bad Reason: When people are unhappy, they often try to make themselves feel better by indulging in addictions or behaviors that may feel good in the moment but are ultimately detrimental. They seek the highs that come from drugs, alcohol, excessive sex, "retail therapy," compulsive gambling, over-eating, and too much television-watching, to name a few. This kind of "happiness" is hardly happiness at all. It is only a temporary way to numb or escape our unhappiness through fleeting experiences of pleasure.

Happy for Good Reason: This is what people usually mean by happiness: having good relationships with our family and friends, success in our careers, financial security, a nice house or car, or using our talents and strengths well. It's the pleasure we derive from having the healthy things in our lives that we want.

Don't get me wrong. I'm all for this kind of happiness! It's just that it's only half the story. Being Happy for Good Reason depends on the external conditions of our lives—these conditions change or are lost, our happiness usually goes too. Relying solely on this type of happiness is where a lot of our fear is stemming from these days. We're afraid the things we think we need to be happy may be slipping from our grasp.

Deep inside, I think we all know that life isn't meant to be about getting by, numbing our pain, or having everything "under control." True happiness doesn't come from merely collecting an assortment of happy experiences. At our core, we know there's something more than this.

There is. It's the next level on the happiness continuum—Happy for No Reason.

Happy for No Reason: This is true happiness—a state of peace and well-being that isn't dependent on external circumstances.

Happy for No Reason isn't elation, euphoria, mood spikes, or peak experiences that don't last. It doesn't mean grinning like a fool 24/7 or experiencing a superficial high. Happy for No Reason isn't an emotion. In fact, when you are Happy for No Reason, you can have *any* emotion—including sadness, fear, anger or hurt—but you still experience that underlying state of peace and well-being.

When you're Happy for No Reason, you *bring* happiness to your outer experiences rather than trying to *extract* happiness from them. You don't need to manipulate the world around you to try to make yourself happy. You live from happiness, rather than *for* happiness.

This is a revolutionary concept. Most of us focus on being Happy for Good Reason, stringing together as many happy experiences as we can, like beads in a necklace, to create a happy life. We have to spend a lot of time and energy trying to find just the right beads so we can have a "happy necklace".

Being Happy for No Reason, in our necklace analogy, is like having a happy string. No matter what beads we put on our necklace—good, bad or indifferent—our inner experience, which is the string that runs through them all, is happy, and creates a happy life.

Happy for No Reason is a state that's been spoken of in virtually all spiritual and religious traditions throughout history. The concept is universal. In Buddhism, it is called causeless joy; in Christianity, the kingdom of Heaven within; and in Judaism it is called *ashrei*, an inner sense of holiness and health. In Islam it is called *falah*, happiness and well-being; and in Hinduism it is called *ananda*, or pure bliss. Some traditions refer to it as an enlightened or awakened state.

So how can you be Happy for No Reason?

Science is verifying the way. Researchers in the field of positive psychology have found that we each have a "happiness set-point," that determines our level of happiness. No matter what happens, whether it's something as exhilarating as winning the lottery or as challenging as a horrible accident, most people eventually return to their original happiness level. Like your weight set-point, which keeps the scale hovering around the same number, your happiness set-point will remain the same **unless you make a concerted effort to change it.** In the same way you'd crank up the thermostat to get comfortable on a chilly day, you actually have the power to reprogram your happiness set-point to a higher level of peace and well-being. The secret lies in practicing the habits of happiness.

Some books and programs will tell you that you can simply decide to be happy. They say just make up your mind to be happy—and you will be.

I don't agree.

You can't just decide to be happy, any more than you can decide to be fit or to be a great piano virtuoso and expect instant mastery. You can, however, decide to take the necessary steps, like exercising or taking piano lessons—and by practicing those skills, you can get in shape or give recitals. In the same way, you can become Happy for No Reason through practicing the habits of happy people.

All of your habitual thoughts and behaviors in the past have created specific neural pathways in the wiring in your brain, like grooves in a record. When we think or behave a certain way over and over, the neural pathway is strengthened and the groove becomes deeper—the way a well-traveled route through a field eventually becomes a clear-cut path. Unhappy people tend to have more negative neural pathways. This is why you can't just ignore the realities of your brain's wiring and *decide* to be happy! To raise your level of happiness, you have to create new grooves.

Scientists used to think that once a person reached adulthood, the brain was fairly well "set in stone" and there wasn't much you could do to change it. But new research is revealing exciting information about the brain's neuroplasticity: when you think, feel and act in different ways, the brain changes and actually rewires itself. You aren't doomed to the same negative neural pathways for your whole life. Leading brain researcher Dr. Richard Davidson, of the University of Wisconsin says, "Based on what we know of the plasticity of the brain, we can think of things like happiness and compassion as skills that are no different from learning to play a musical instrument or tennis .... it is possible to train our brains to be happy."

While a few of the Happy 100 I interviewed were born happy, most of them learned to be happy by practicing habits that supported their happiness. That means wherever you are on the happiness continuum, it's entirely in your power to raise your happiness level.

In the course of my research, I uncovered 21 core happiness habits that anyone can use to become happier and stay that way. You can find all 21 happiness habits at www.HappyForNoReason.com

Here are a few tips to get you started:

1. **Incline Your Mind Toward Joy.** Have you noticed that your mind tends to register the negative events in your life more than the positive? If you get ten compliments in a day and one criticism, what do you remember? For most people, it's the criticism. Scientists call this our "negativity bias" — our primitive survival wiring that causes us to pay more attention to the negative than the positive. To reverse this bias, get into the daily habit of consciously registering the positive around you: the sun on your skin, the taste of a favorite food, a smile or kind word from a co-worker or friend. Once you notice something positive, take a moment to savor it deeply and feel it; make it more than just a mental observation. Spend 20 seconds soaking up the happiness you feel.

2. **Let Love Lead.** One way to power up your heart's flow is by sending loving kindness to your friends and family, as well as strangers you pass on the street. Next time you're waiting for the elevator at work, stuck in a line at the store or caught up in traffic, send a silent wish to the people you see for their happiness, well-being, and health. Simply wishing others well switches on the "pump" in your own heart that generates love and creates a strong current of happiness.

3. **Lighten Your Load.** To make a habit of letting go of worries and negative thoughts, start by letting go on the physical level. Cultural anthropologist Angeles Arrien recommends giving or throwing away 27 items a day for nine days. This deceptively simple practice will help you break attachments that no longer serve you.

4. **Make Your Cells Happy.** Your brain contains a veritable pharmacopeia of natural happiness-enhancing neurochemicals — endorphins, serotonin, oxytocin, and dopamine — just waiting to be released to every organ and cell in your body. The way that you eat, move, rest, and even your facial expression can shift the balance of your body's feel-good-chemicals, or "Joy Juice", in your favor. To dispense some extra Joy Juice — smile. Scientists have discovered that smiling decreases stress hormones and boosts happiness chemicals, which increase the body's T-cells, reduce pain, and enhance relaxation. You may not feel like it, but smiling — even artificially to begin with — starts the ball rolling and will turn into a real smile in short order.

5. **Hang with the Happy.** We catch the emotions of those around us just like we catch their colds — it's called emotional contagion. So it's important to make wise choices about the company you keep. Create appropriate boundaries with emotional bullies and "happiness vampires" who suck the life out of you. Develop your happiness "dream team" — a mastermind or support group you meet with regularly to keep you steady on the path of raising your happiness.

"Happily ever after" isn't just for fairytales or for only the lucky few. Imagine experiencing inner peace and well-being as the backdrop for everything else in your life. When you're Happy for No Reason, it's not that your life always looks perfect — it's that, however it looks, you'll still be happy!

By Marci Shimoff. Based on the New York Times bestseller *Happy for No Reason: 7 Steps to Being Happy from the Inside Out*, which offers a revolutionary approach to experiencing deep and lasting happiness. The woman's face of the *Chicken Soup for the Soul* series and a featured teacher in *The Secret*, Marci is an authority on success, happiness, and the law of attraction. To order *Happy for No Reason* and receive free bonus gifts, go to www.happyfornoreason.com/mybook.

Sex, Love and Relationships

DR. JOHN GRAY

Just as great sex is important to lasting love, good health is important to sex and relationships. About 12 years ago, I cured myself of early stage Parkinson's disease. The doctors were amazed, but my wife was even more amazed. She noted that our relationship and sex life had become dramatically better. It turns out that the natural supplements I used to reverse Parkinson's can also make you more attentive and loving in your relationship. At that point, I realized that good relationship skills alone were not enough to sustain love and passion for a lifetime.

I shared many insights gained from my 40 years' experience as a marriage counselor and coach in *Men Are From Mars, Women Are From Venus*. And while my insights go a long way towards helping men and women understand and support each other, good communication skills alone are not always enough. For better relationships, we not only need to be healthy, but we must also experience optimum brain function.

If you are tired, depressed, anxious, not sleeping well, or in pain, then certainly romantic feelings will become a thing of the past. My recovery from Parkinson's revealed to me the profound connection between the quality of our health and our relationships. This insight has motivated me, over the past twelve years, to research the secrets of optimum health as a foundation for lasting love.

These are health secrets that are generally not explored in medical school. In medical school, doctors are indoctrinated into the culture of examining the symptoms, identifying the sickness, and prescribing a drug to treat that sickness. They learn very little about how to be healthy or to sustain successful relationships.

There are no university courses entitled "Better Nutrition For Better Sex". Drugs sometimes save lives, but they also have negative side effects that do little to preserve the passion in a relationship. Ideally, drugs should be used as a last resort and 90 % of our health plan should be drug free. From this perspective, the heath care crisis, as well as our high rate of divorce in America, is indirectly caused by our dependence on doctors and prescription drugs.

Most people have not even considered that taking prescribed drugs (even for the small stuff) can weaken their relationships, which in turn makes them more vulnerable to more disease. For example, if you are feeling depressed or anxious, a drug may numb your pain, but it does nothing to help you correct the cause of your problem. It can even prevent you from feeling your natural motivation to get the emotional support you need. In a variety of ways, our common health complaints are all expressions of two major conditions: our lack of education to identify and support unmet gender-specific emotional needs; and our lack of education to identify and support unmet gender-specific nutritional needs.

With an understanding of natural solutions that have been around for thousands of years, drugs are not needed to treat many common complaints. Some symptoms like low energy, weight gain, allergies, hormonal imbalance, mood swings, poor sleep, indigestion, lack of focus, ADD and ADHD, procrastination, low motivation, memory loss, decreased libido, PMS, vaginal dryness, muscle and joint pain, or the lack of passion in life and/or our relationships can be treated drug-free. By using drugs (even over-the-counter drugs) to treat these common complaints, our bodies and relationships are weakened, making us more vulnerable to bigger and more costly health challenges like cancer, diabetes, heart disease, auto-immune disease, dementia, and Alzheimer's. In simple terms, by handling the easy stuff (the common complaints) without doctors and drugs, we can protect ourselves from the big stuff (cancer, heart disease, dementia, etc.) We can be healthy and also enjoy lasting love and passion in our personal lives.

Even if you are taking anti-depressants or hormone replacement therapy, sometimes all it takes to stop treating the symptom is to directly handle the cause. With specific mineral orotates (something most people have never heard of) or omega three oil from the brains of salmon, your stress levels immediately drop and you begin to feel happy and in love again.

For every health challenge, we have explored the effects on our relationships, as well as with natural remedies that can sometimes produce immediate positive results. You can find these natural solutions to common health complaints for free at my website: www.MarsVenus.com.

What they don't teach in medical school is how to be healthy and happy without the use of drugs or hormone replacement. By refusing drugs and taking responsibility for your health, a wealth of new possibilities can become available to you. We are designed to be healthy and happy, and it is within our reach if we commit to increasing our knowledge.

New research regarding the brain differences in men and women reveals how specific nutritional supplements, combined with gender-specific relationship and self-nurturing skills, can stimulate the hormones of health, happiness and increased energy. Over the past 10 years in my healing center in California, I witnessed how natural solutions coupled with gender-specific relationship skills could solve our common health complaints without drugs. By addressing these common complaints without prescribed drugs, not only do we feel better, but our relationships have the potential to improve dramatically.

Ultimately the cause of all our common complaints is higher stress levels. Researchers around the world all agree that chronic stress levels in our bodies provide a basis for any and all disease to take hold. An easy and quick solution for lowering our stress reactions is specific nutritional support combined with gender-smart relationship skills. Extra nutritional support is needed because stress depletes the body very quickly of essential nutrients. When a car engine is running more quickly, it uses fuel more quickly. When we are stressed, we need both extra nutrients and extra emotional support. Understanding what we need to take and where to get it requires education. Every week day at www.MarsVenus.com I have a live daily show where I freely answer questions and provide this much-needed new gender-specific insight.

At www.MarsVenus.com, we are happy to share what we have learned for creating healthy bodies and positive relationships. You can find a host of natural solutions for common complaints and feel confident that you have the power to feel fully alive with an abundance of energy and positive feelings that will enrich all your relationships.

Inspiring Leaders to Make a Difference

DR. WENDY SNEDDON

I wanted to change the *world*.

When I was young, I wanted to change the *world*,

I found it was difficult to change the *world*, so I tried to change my *community*.

When I found, I couldn't change my community; I began to focus on my *business*.

Now I realise the only thing I can change is *myself*,

Suddenly I realise that if I change *myself*,

I could have an impact on my *business*.

My *business* and I could make an impact on my *community*,

Then my *community* and I will indeed change the *world*.

Wendy's Version. Original Written
by an unknown Monk around 1100 A.D.

Have you ever worked for a great leader who is both encouraging and challenges you both at the same time? In 2012, I found myself in that situation. One year into this job and it was time for my first appraisal. Like most people, I was very nervous because you never know how it was going to go, but my employer quickly put me at ease, and it was a productive time.

Towards the end, he said to me, "I don't know how you are going to do it, but I want to be in The Sunday Times top 100 best small businesses to work for." This is a published list that UK companies can get onto and it is managed by The Sunday Times. I eagerly took on the challenge, but when I did my research and found out what it was going to take, well let's just say that I had serious doubts about the feasibility of it.

Much of it had to do with how our employees saw our company and most of them were not happy working for us. We had a fractured company based over 14 sites, and their only support was through me. How could we ever get the 3 Star "Extraordinary" rating required to be even considered for the list?

This wasn't a matter of changing a few known things. I had to start from scratch and figure out why they were unhappy and then come up with a solution that would not only solve the problem, but do it in such a way that our employees would tell others that we were the best to work for. There were times it felt like an impossible task.

BUT...

If there is one thing I have learned over my years of experience, it's that if you are willing to tackle a project head on and believe in your employees, anything is possible. So, I started by figuring out where the problem was and for that I designed a Happiness Survey. From that survey, I learned two things:

1. Most of the employees were not happy with their managers and how they were treated.

2. Communication across the entire company was poor. People felt disconnected and unappreciated for their hard work.

Now that I knew the problems, I could come up with solutions to help position us to be on that coveted list. Over the next six months, I implemented activities that would improve both areas.

I started with a weekly newsletter called Briefly Connected. We collected news from around the practices – I got people to send me interesting stories, shared people's birthdays and anniversaries and highlighted different people in this weekly e-bulletin and that became quite popular.

To connect people even more, I organised a company-wide conference where all employees came together for an entire weekend, where they received training and a special Awards Dinner which had a focus on recognition.

As I looked at the managers, I realised that this was an important area that would need a lot of focus. They were all excellent at their job but required training in management. As a result of this, I designed a leadership program for each manager in the practice as we recognised that people were unhappy with their managers and the way they were managed. Every two months we got the managers together, performed leadership and management training with them and gave them support so that they knew what to do when they went back to their teams.

Guess what?

When I had the employees do another Happiness Survey six months later, the results had greatly improved. So much so I felt we were in a position where we could actually move forward and go for the top 100 list and that year we made #48 and have been on that list, every year since.

A GREAT LEADER MAKES ALL THE DIFFERENCE

While there are many contributing factors to a successful company, one of the main ones is the excellence of the leader, because they set the pace for everything that happens.

How can you recognise a great leader? A great leader is someone who shares responsibility for running the business with the team. They give regular feedback on all aspects of the business. They look for areas where they can support, develop and do further training on areas that are needed, while always encouraging their team to go the extra mile.

They care about their employees and their lives. One leader I know, knew all of his employee's names, their partners' and kid's names as well. He remembered little things about them, so when he went in to visit people, he would ask them about their family life, everyone felt like they really knew him. People appreciated that he took the time to remember things about them and the initiatives he put in place, so in turn worked harder to make the company great.

TODAY'S LEADERS

The majority of leaders these days can be selfish and focus on their own position in the business and where they are going and expect everyone to do what they need them to do. I have known leaders who expect everyone to work their socks off, so they can reap the rewards.

A friend of mine had an experience where her boss had to reach a certain sales goal by the end of the year and promised that if it was reached there would be a specific reward given. My friend and the other employee worked day and night to reach that goal, and in the final few hours of the year, they did it. They were so happy and eagerly awaited their reward, but it never came. The boss got his reward and recognition, but this was never reciprocated.

After that experience, she felt demotivated, and the next time the employer promised a reward neither my friend nor the other employee even tried to work for it because they knew it was a lie.

Leaders need to keep their word and show that they are investing back into the company to reward the people, which in turn motivates employees to do more.

Many company owners are great technicians. They understand what they do, what they make or what they build, but they lack other skills (such as people, marketing or financial skills) and often don't recognize it. They try to do everything themselves and they don't know how to do many of the tasks well. They are afraid to admit that they don't know everything and they are often afraid to trust someone else to do this. They think that they are the only ones who can do it right. They have problems with delegation, and they don't want to let go of that control.

When employees are not trusted, or allowed to think freely and contribute to the business, they don't feel valued as a member of the team, and in return, they just come to work and go home again and are much less productive. They take more sick time and stress leave. They tend to be negative and drag other people down. This causes a high transfer rate of employees in and out, which is a huge cost to the business. All these things affect the overall profit and the viability of the business.

20 THINGS GREAT LEADERS ENSURE

If you check out some of the best small to medium size businesses today, you will see that they are run by leaders who all exhibit similar qualities and consistently ensure that all of the company's needs, including those of the employees, are met. Let's look at twenty of the most common qualities of leaders:

1. Vision

Great leaders have a clear vision of where they want the company to go and what they want the business to achieve. Along with that is the ability to communicate their vision to everyone in the company, so they understand how their roles in the business contribute to the overall success.

2. Passion

It is important to be passionate about your business. To love what you do as a leader and to inspire everyone around you to feel passionate about it too.

3. Transparency and Integrity

If you say you are going to do something, then you do it, no matter what. If you lose integrity with your employees, you will find that they will no longer go out of their way for you. Transparency about the performance of the company is also an important element.

4. Listener

Great leaders are good listeners and will act on what they hear. They need to be willing to do things like surveys and then be prepared to make changes. They can accept negative comments, learn some things about themselves and then change some things about the way that they behave.

Good listening skills include being aware of what is going on in the team, which means getting to know what is going on for people at work and outside of work, so when things aren't going so well you can spot it. This means when poor performance is going on you can pick up on it quickly and do something about it.

5. Communicate

You need to have systems for communication in place. How does information such as policies, training, and recognition get conveyed in a way that everyone who needs to hear it, does so? This is important for the productivity of the company, whether that's setting up a Facebook group, using a LinkedIn group or having an internal newsletter. It is important to find a way that works for everybody, to make sure that they all get the same messages.

6. Believe That People Behave with Positive Intentions

A good leader believes that the people in their team do things with positive intentions. This cancels out a blame culture where it is everyone else's fault when something goes wrong. Belief is powerful in that people will live up to what you believe in them. If you believe them to be good, hardworking employees, who occasionally make fixable mistakes they work towards that. If you believe the opposite, then they live to that too.

If you create an environment where you work with your employees to fix mistakes, without playing the blame game, you will find your employees are more willing to come to you with problems instead of hiding them, and the problems can then be resolved more quickly instead of being left.

7. Responsibility

Give people responsibility, then empower them to do their job and to let them get on with it. Give them a clear brief of what outcome you want to see. Let the person go away and do the job in the way that they want to do it and as long as the outcome is what is expected, how the job is performed shouldn't really matter. This gives employees the freedom to develop things in their own way.

8. Reward and Recognise

A good leader should have a system of rewards and recognition. These can be quite difficult to implement because employers and managers tend to have their favourites. Therefore, any system has to be transparent, easy to understand, and be able to achieve that reward and recognition.

One place I worked at had a great reward system where we gave out everyone 'Alfies.' These were like pound notes, with a picture of Alfie, the owner's dog on the front, and on the back of it, you wrote who you were giving it to and what they had done to help you and inspire you. You signed your name and gave it to someone to say thank you. At the end of the year, you could cash them in for money or vouchers or gifts.

The emphasis was on looking out for the good things that people had done and then telling them about it by saying, "Thank you". This helped to improve the culture because people were looking for the positive qualities in others.

9. Fair Compensation

Properly compensating your employees for the work they do should never be considered a cost but instead an investment with a great return on investment. If you want to build an amazing team of loyal, hard working people who want to make your company succeed, then be generous with wages and the benefits that you offer.

10. Deal with Conflicts

How do good leaders resolve conflict? They deal with them quickly. They don't let things fester, and as a result they will go in and sort things out at the earliest opportunity. They also create a culture where people feel comfortable to come forward and talk about any issues.

11. Open to New Ideas

A great leader is open to employees coming forward with ideas and then taking some of those ideas and letting it be part of the vision of the company. Letting the employee work on the project where appropriate can also prove to be a powerful motivational tool

12. Be Yourself

Authenticity. You don't have to be perfect. Admitting concerns and flaws and getting help from the team is a sign of strength, not weakness. Encourage your team to come up with solutions to problems.

13. Flexible

Be open minded and flexible. You should have a 5-year plan, but you also need to be able to adapt this if the financial climate changes (such as the uncertainties around Brexit). You also have to be open to adapting to technology that comes along.

14. Positivity

Create a culture of optimism by encouraging people to make the impossible possible. You set the tone for your company and its employees, so make it a good one.

15. Commitment

When your employees know that you are committed to the success of the company and them personally, they will become committed to the company as well.

16. Training

Invest in training. First for yourself. Learn the practical elements of leading a team, but there is also that personal element where leaders need to learn to recognize their own behaviours: the way they communicate, their preferences and they really have to work on themselves first. Once you have changed yourself, you can develop a culture of personal growth and learning with your employees.

17. Being Honest About the Financial Data

Share the figures with your team. Get people to understand what the top line is, what the bottom line needs to be and what activities are going to help the company to get there. Help them understand where every penny in the pound goes and that sometimes at the end there is not much left over. They need to know how to control costs and maximise fails so that there is money to send people for training and to do rewards.

18. Understand Work/Life Balance

Do not expect people to work day and night and put systems in place so that they don't have to. Respect people's personal time and ensure they get it. Do not expect people to work extremely long hours, be on call and then work the next day. If it is required then ensure they are thanked and adequately compensated.

19. Well Being

Have a well-being policy. Set up a committee to look at all aspects of this and what is needed and what is not. Have a stress policy, carry out a survey to assess how your team manages stress. How can you help your employees feel better about work and create a healthy environment for them to work in?

20. Dedication

Your dedication is what is going to make the company work. If the boss doesn't care, then others won't either. The tone must be set from the top and then allowed to flow down through the company.

THE BEST STARTING PLACE

What a list! It may feel like a lot to live up to; the great thing is that you don't have to implement this all at once. It can take place over time. One of the best places to start is being clear about the vision of your business.

When it is just you, it is easy to have a vision and work within it, but when you start to bring in other people, it becomes more complicated. Having a clear goal of where you want to go with your company is a good place to start and explaining this to your new team helps them to understand what you want to achieve. Next, consider what you want the team culture to look like and how you want them to behave. The best time to design your ideal culture is before you have a team, but it is never too late to start.

One thing I strongly encourage you to do is to get the training and support you need to be a great leader. Very few people can successfully do it on their own and you are setting yourself up for failure if you think you can.

But what support is out there for leaders like you? Many training courses are designed for large companies with huge budgets and massive HR Departments to implement the ideas shared. What about small to medium sized businesses? Shouldn't they be able to benefit from training designed to help them and their employees?

Wouldn't it be great to work with someone who understands where you are as an employer and help YOU come with a custom plan that:

1. Helps you to identify the problems.

2. Looks at feasible solutions.

3. Creates a custom solution that fits your budget.

Well, you can. My company Lodestone Lounge was created for entrepreneurs by entrepreneurs. We specialise in helping you:

- With leadership coaching

- Attract & recruit the right people

- Provide the right environment for your team to develop

- Offer your team the rights and protections they're guaranteed by law

- Keep up to date with changes to legislation

- Have access to the latest and best HR advice through relevant websites and our in-house HR and legal team

- Provide your team with legal and relevant contracts of employment

- Write policies, procedures, and handbooks which work for your business and your team

- Have the HR software you need, tailored to your business, at your fingertips with our Great Employee Management System (GEMS).

Go to www.LodestoneLounge.com to find out how my company can help your company achieve its true potential.

The choice is yours.

Real Estate Isn't Just A Man's Game

5 Key Tips for Women Investors

CORA CRISTOBAL

Are you someone who wants to start investing in real estate, but doesn't know where to start? Are you someone who's trying to get back into it after failing at it once? Are you a semi-experienced investor looking to improve your returns?

If you answered "yes" to any of the above questions, then I commend you! Real estate investing is a very rewarding field, as long as you know what you're doing. In fact, at the lowest point in my life, the real estate market helped me get back on my feet and turn my life around for good.

Approximately ten years ago, I divorced my husband. Since his income was nearly twice as much as mine, our separation meant that I had to start living a lot more scarcely, until I could find a way to replace the income that he provided for me. And that's precisely what I did.

I started by transforming my basement into a pair of makeshift bedrooms so that I could rent them out at a profit. Once I got the hang of that, I invested in condos in Canada, rented them for income, and then flipped them for a profit after a few years. Then, I bought cheap American properties and rented those out, expanding my income even more. Before long, I had worked my way up to other money-making opportunities, and I was living more comfortably. As of now, I'm even better off than when I was married.

To me, real estate wasn't just a source of income, but a source of proof that I didn't have to depend on a man to live the life I wanted. On top of that, I proved that a single woman is perfectly capable of making it in a male-dominated industry.

Ultimately, I decided that my divorce wasn't going to be the end of my life; it was going to be a new beginning. And it can be a new beginning for you, too!

But that doesn't mean that real estate investing is easy. In fact, there are several pitfalls that I've seen countless novice investors fall into. Before you start your new career path, you should familiarize yourself with the most common (and often the most dangerous) mistakes made by new investors, so that you can avoid making them yourself.

MISTAKE #1
FALLING IN LOVE WITH THE PROPERTY

One thing you have to keep in mind is that you're looking for a property to rent out, not a property to live in. You need to look for the neighborhood that's experiencing the greatest demand, rather than the one that's most suited to your tastes.

The metrics you would use to choose a property to live in aren't identical to the metrics you'd use to choose one to rent. True, both decisions involve choosing a property that's centered in a good neighborhood, with close proximity to decent schools, shopping centers, and hospitals. However, there are several factors that are relevant to renters but not to buyers. Return on Investment (ROI), for instance, is the ratio between the income you receive from rent payments and the cost of the property. In other words, it measures how much you'll earn from the property compared to how much you had to pay for it. (If you were simply looking for a place to live, this wouldn't be a concern.)

By the same token, qualities that you look for in a home may not necessarily be qualities that make it rentable. If you plan on having children, you may base your judgment on whether the home is suitable for raising a family. As an investor, however, this cannot become the deciding factor in your decision, since a home without enough space for a four-person family can still be perfectly rentable to a single woman, a recent college graduate or an elderly couple. Don't limit your options.

Furthermore, you can't let yourself get too attached to the property you're investing in. You have to keep reminding yourself that, ultimately, you're going to have to part ways with the house and leave it in the hands of somebody else.

The point is, the factors that need to be at the front of your mind are the ones that determine whether the property can be rented out at a profit. Remember, you're not looking for a house that's good for you; you're looking for a property that's appealing to the average consumer.

MISTAKE #2
DISREGARDING SHORT-TERM CASH FLOW

When you're choosing a property to buy to rent, you may be tempted to look at projections on whether the property is expected to appreciate in value over time. That's fine if you want to keep the information in the back of your mind, but it shouldn't be your first priority. That needs to be short-term passive, positive cash flow, or how much you'll earn from rent payments in the coming months.

After all, making money through a resale requires time. It can take years or even decades for a house to appreciate significantly in value. In the meantime, you're going to need a way to feed, clothe and sustain yourself on a day-to-day basis.

Furthermore, projections aren't guarantees. There are so many different factors outside of our control that affect the housing market; nobody, not even experts like myself, can say with absolute certainty what a house's value will be ten to twenty years from now. Why base your decision on a projected increase in profit that could very well be nullified by a downturn in the market that nobody saw coming?

There's nothing wrong with planning for the far future per se, but planning for the near future is considerably more important. It's better to go for a smaller reward that you're guaranteed to receive immediately than to go for a large reward that you may or may not receive after a while. Remember, a bird in the hand is worth two in the bush.

MISTAKE #3
STARTING TOO BIG

Let's say you want to teach yourself how to cook. You don't start with fancy, elaborate recipes that take hours to prepare, do you? Of course not; you'd just end up ruining your dinner or even your kitchen. Instead, you start with simple recipes, and once you've mastered those, you gradually work your way up to the harder stuff.

Why should real estate investing be any different? All too often, I've seen new investors immediately set their eyes on fancy, expensive multi-million dollar properties. While those kinds of properties have a chance of offering a huge return for you, it's also incredibly likely that you'll suffer a huge loss, especially if you don't have the discerning, savvy eye of an experienced investor.

Instead, start by investing in smaller properties within the $100K-$500K range. In fact, you can start even smaller than that by renting out rooms in your living space (like I did). Some investors start by purchasing a small duplex property to live in and then renting out one of the units to someone else, thus fulfilling their need for a source of income and a roof over their head at the same time.

Then, once you've saved up enough money from rent payments, you can work your way up to larger houses. Slowly, but surely, you can increase the value of what you buy, and consequently, increase your income. As I mentioned above, that was how I broke into the real estate industry, and it worked wonders for me.

Of course, if you don't trust your own judgment, you may be interested in forming a partnership with another investor. Which leads me to my next point.

MISTAKE #4
CHOOSING THE WRONG PARTNER

A partnership, on its own, isn't a bad idea; in fact, it can be a very good one. There are lots of advantages to forming a partnership with another investor. Ideally, you'll have someone with whom to share the workload, and an extra source of knowledge and expertise. Plus, you'll have the potential to make more capital without investing as much of your personal funds or getting too much credit.

Note, however, that I said "ideally." In a worst-case scenario, you'll end up with a partner who never does their share, makes bad decisions on your behalf, and almost ruins your chances of ever making it as an investor. If you want to avoid that (and I assume that you do), there are a few things you will have to keep in mind before you decide to make your partnership official.

First of all, if you plan on forming a partnership with someone else, it needs to be someone who knows what they're doing, or at least someone who doesn't know any less than you do. Check their credentials and see if they have any background in real estate or any form of investment planning. If you're new to the field, you don't want to end up in a "blind leading the blind" situation.

Second of all, you have to find someone whose goals are more or less the same as yours. Remember, your primary objective is maximizing passive, positive cash flow, so make sure that your partner's looking for the same thing. Otherwise, it'll be almost impossible to find an investment plan that satisfies both your needs.

For this reason, I strongly suggest putting every agreement in writing. Discuss every course of action thoroughly, and once you reach a consensus, put it down on a piece of paper and sign it. I've seen too many partners mistakenly assume that they were "on the same page," only to pay dearly for it later.

Furthermore, holding regular discussions is a great way to familiarize yourself with the field. You'll be exposed to a separate point of view, you'll learn to use real estate lingo properly, and most importantly, you'll end up making better decisions than you would have on your own. Two heads are better than one, after all.

MISTAKE #5
GOING IN WITHOUT A MENTOR

A partner is, for all intents and purposes, your equal, and she has a direct stake in your decision-making process. For a truly reliable source of guidance, you're going to need someone far more knowledgeable than yourself, who can evaluate your situation from a non-biased perspective.

I may have accomplished a lot, but I didn't get to where I am entirely on my own, although I tried. For several years, I tried to tackle the real estate industry alone, and as a result, things didn't go as smoothly as I had hoped. In fact, many of the mistakes I've outlined in this chapter are mistakes that I made in my early years. Things improved for me when I hired a mentor. He had experience investing in both Canada and the United States, and he was willing to share all of the high and low points of his career with me: the failures and successes. By telling me of his failures, he taught me what to avoid doing as an investor. By telling me of his successes, he imbued me with the confidence to carry on; if he could do it, I could do it too.

After a few years of meeting with my mentor twice a month, I had both the knowledge to avoid making bad decisions and the confidence to make good ones. Also, I was able to invest in my personal growth and development. I established and improved my brand; that contributed largely to my success.

I'm proud of my success, but I would have earned it a lot sooner if I had hired a mentor from the very beginning. So, don't repeat the biggest mistake I made in my career — starting without a muse.

If you're interested in learning more about my coaching, mentoring or consulting services, please visit www.TorontoWomensClub.com or feel free to contact me at cora.cristobal@gmail.com.

Control Money Before Money Controls You

K. RAJ SINGH

My aim in contributing to this book is to inspire and motivate others through sharing my experiences – both successes and failures. My hope for you is that after reading, you realize you are just as, or even more, capable of becoming successful and having financial freedom as I have had the fortune to be. Don't get me wrong; I have had to overcome multiple obstacles in order to end up where I am in life. I believe that we don't go through mishaps and failures solely to benefit ourselves, but also so that we can impart our wisdom upon the general public and benefit humanity's quality of life as a whole.

My drive and ambition stems from growing up in a single parent household with my mother and sister. Early on in life, my parents divorced and I was given the role of man of the house. I soon found that with that title came responsibility – responsibility to provide for my family, support my family, and secure a stable financial future. Throughout this time, my ambition was in the background, ever-fueling and driving my desire for more. I wanted more for my future, more for my family, but not just in a financial sense. I've heard of so many families that struggle not financially, but emotionally, because the provider was continuously absent due to their efforts to secure a stable lifestyle for their family. I didn't want to impart that emotional burden on my family. I wanted to be there for them and not just function as their savings account or an invisible man who allows them to live a comfortable life. I wanted to be there for my sister's graduation, or my child's first steps and first words. I wanted to be present.

Being a good person and being successful are not mutually exclusive characteristics, but neither do they come hand in hand. You can be a genuinely good human being in terms of honesty and generosity, but not accomplished in terms of achieving your career goals. In order to become who I wanted to be for my family, I had to learn how to be both the best and most successful person I had the potential to be. To do this, I attended multiple seminars and workshops on personal development, investing, and financial success. To this day, I still continue to learn and grow as a person with every day I live, but one seminar has had a significant impact on my financial life, specifically. This was Peak Potentials' Millionaire Mind Intensive by T. Harv Eker (now called New Peaks' Millionaire Mind Experience*). The Millionaire Mind Intensive seminar taught me not to just wonder why life is the way it is and imagine my position in life as static, but to start asking myself how I could change my financial blueprint and future. And that's exactly what I did.

I am now in a global mastermind group with New Peaks and feel blessed to have been able to spend time with the CEO, Adam Markel, who is also author of the book Pivot. I've visited him in his home in California, where we spent hours brainstorming ideas and solutions for our businesses, while also making time for fun and giving back to a worthy cause with our time and physical labor. The dedication that Mr. Markel and the rest of his team put into their company is wondrous and admirable. I, along with countless other people, have taken many of the courses and retreats they offer – my favorite being the Enlightened Warrior Training Camp. The name alone says a lot about the focus of the retreat as becoming an enlightened warrior means to conquer oneself.

As I mentioned before, I wanted to figure out a way to be financially successful but also be present for my family. The best way I have found to do this was to delegate and relinquish some control. For some people this may be hard, especially the types that are perfectionists and relish the ability to oversee every detail of any operation. But in order for me to have enough free time to spend with my family and loved ones, I had to realize that a significant amount of the work I did myself could be distributed and done by other people. I began to hire others to do the more routine work I had grown accustomed to doing myself and although at first glance this seemed like a big initial investment, I soon reaped its benefits. Not having to do the work of multiple people allowed me to focus on the more complex aspects of the projects I was working on and with greater focus came increased levels of productivity. That's when the successes started rolling in.

None of the headway I made after bringing in others to help would have been possible if I hadn't realized the importance of continued education, even after obtaining my Bachelor's Degree. This doesn't necessarily have to mean taking online classes or auditing courses at your local college – it can be as simple as reading an article on a topic you don't know much about or taking a weekend and attending a seminar on smart investing. Having a vast store of a variety of information allows you to be creative in your problem solving and future planning, as you can take multiple viewpoints when looking at the situations you find yourself in. "Knowledge is power" isn't a famous quote just because the sound of the words is aurally appealing; there is innate truth in those three words, dating back to 1597 in Sir Francis Bacon's Meditationes Sacrae. As you can see, this book isn't just about investing in stocks or bonds; rather it's about investing in yourself – your education, your future, and your success. To take it a step further, I believe knowledge, when applied, is power. Warren Buffet, the biggest investor of our time, says: "The best investment you can make is an investment in yourself... The more you learn, the more you'll earn." I've noticed throughout my life that wealthy people tend to always have extensive libraries in their homes and I firmly believe there is a correlation between their success and the importance they put on accumulating knowledge. Knowledge, and the ability of correctly applying it, are the greatest assets in the world because the dividends are infinite.

*As a thank you for purchasing this book, I am offering a scholarship certificate for you and a family member to attend the 3-day Millionaire Mind Experience Seminar as my complimentary guests. Valued at $2,590 – free for a limited time! Go to www.thepassiveincomebook.com

THE LAW OF ATTRACTION

The law of attraction ultimately boils down to the idea that "like attracts like." In a way, our thoughts are made up of energy, just as we are, and whether our thoughts are positive or negative can determine whether we encounter positive or negative experiences. The idea of similar energy types attracting each other, also known as the law of attraction, was brought to fame and popularity through Rhonda Byrne's book-turned-movie, The Secret. I was blessed to come across this book at a pivotal point in my life and owe most of my beliefs to the lessons I took from reading it. I truly believe it to be the single most powerful and impactful piece of literature I have studied. When I met the greatest motivational speaker, Anthony Robbins*, I learned that all of us have a vibrational energy, and in order to succeed, we need to increase our energy levels to the maximum we can obtain. The more energy we have, the more of what we want from the universe we can attract. You can think of it in terms of gravity – bigger bodies of matter have bigger gravitational pulls, and ultimately attract larger amounts of mass. The sun is a good example of this. Surrounded by eight planets, a dwarf planet, and countless asteroids, the sun is a giant orb, pulsing of energy and attracting an incredible amount of matter towards it. We should all try to draw as much positive energy towards ourselves as possible.

An efficient way to attract favorable energy is to actively maintain a positive attitude every day. I cannot stress enough how important I have found having a positive attitude to be. Especially since we live in a world where negative happens all around us, this may initially be harder than it seems but with conscious effort, staying positive can become habit. To help you visualize this, I want you to imagine a field of dirt. Without doing anything or putting in any effort, grass and weeds will take it over and destroy its potential. However, by planting your own crops and nurturing them with fertile soil and water, you can eventually end up with a bountiful field full of fruits or vegetables. With effort, the positive has overcome the default negative. In this same way, actively trying to maintain a positive attitude can help you eliminate the negative that regrettably encompasses the world.

A more tangible way to do this in your daily life is to listen to personal development and motivational audio books in your spare time. I used to use the time I spent commuting to work to do this; I even called my car my "University on Wheels." No matter where I was going, I was always able to feel as if I'd done something productive, other than driving from point

A to point B. If audio books aren't up your alley, you could also opt for the real paper version of the books. Reading every night before bed has become a deeply embedded habit for me, and I regard it as a habit everyone should develop. Most people spend their last minutes before sleep watching the news on TV, something full to the brim with negativity. "If it bleeds, it leads" is a common phrase that comes to mind when we think about the news – is that something really the last thing we want to be exposed to before sleeping? Our mind will slowly fade away from consciousness as we fall asleep, but our subconscious is still processing all of the violence and blood we witnessed through the TV. I equate watching the news before bed with letting someone come into your home and throw garbage everywhere right before you leave the house. Don't let something as negative as a newscast filled with misfortune and violence fill your mind right before sleep. Alternatively, think about if you were to just read a few pages of a motivational book before going to bed – the last words you experience before sleep are now something positive and propelling. You wake up feeling refreshed and energized the next morning, ready to tackle whatever challenges you may face that day.

A good tactic I have found for achieving success and a positive attitude is to find a person who is successful in the way you want to be and to study them. As I mentioned before, continuing education is an important part of achieving your goals, and studying people is yet another way you can learn to improve. I've had countless mentors over the years and even a life coach to help me through the happy and more complicated times. Each of these people has impacted my life in different ways, as every one of them had different experiences and types of knowledge to offer. I consciously recognize that without these people, I would be nowhere near the place where I am today. I am also able to realize that not only have these people helped me get to where I am now, but also my past mistakes have been integral to my success.

I firmly stand by the idea that we are all in the right place at the right time. Even though things may seem difficult at that specific time, or you may fail once or twice or several times, everything that happens to you is meant to happen. No matter the situation, there is always a lesson you can learn from your experiences.

Your income will never exceed your self-image of how great you perceive yourself to be, therefore you must grow your self-image alongside self-improvement to feel truly worthy of a greater income. In order to better visualize my goals, I created a vision board. A vision board can be something as simple as a poster with pictures of things you want in your future, regardless of what facet of life they pertain to. I love staring at my vision board and feeling excited about living in that reality. I encourage everyone to ponder over their vision board every day and visualize living that life in the present so you can attract it. It's a rewarding feeling that I can't properly put into words when you're able to start watching yourself achieve those goals and subsequently replacing them with new dreams. Some of the things I've achieved from my vision board are owning a new Mercedes Benz, meeting Billionaire Sir Richard Branson* at the iconic Playboy Mansion, meeting Mogul P. Diddy*, having a library for others to learn from, invited to Tai Lopez's $16 Million Mansion in Beverly Hills*, owning different passive income businesses I'll discuss later in the chapter, and so many more.

Going along with the idea that exuding positive energy attracts more positive energy, I believe that gratitude is one of the most powerful forces of the universe. Being grateful in life attracts more things to be grateful for. I believe if the ability to feel gratitude is not learned on the way up, then it will surely be learned on the way down. To make sure I have agency in expressing and being aware of the things I'm grateful for, I often write in my Gratitude Journal before I go to sleep at night. Essentially it is a list of all the things I feel blessed to have in life overall, specifically for that day, and specifically in that moment.

Unfortunately, most people are used to thinking about all the things in life they are unhappy about. They subsequently focus on and put passion into those things to try and fix them which is a recipe for more disaster. Rather than counting their blessings, they're counting their problems. Once you find a way to deliberately focus on all of your blessings, more of them will come to you and you will ultimately be happier in life. As I like to say, "the Pessimist may be more accurate, but the Optimist lives longer and happier."

A way that I have found to remain positive and focused on my blessings is having sessions with my life coach, whom I've had for over a decade now. Our sessions have consisted of a half an hour phone call every 2 weeks for over the last 10 years. My life coach, Dr. Elena Pezzini, helps me to set realistic goals and holds me accountable to them. She also is always making sure all areas of my life are in balanced harmony with each other and steers me in the right direction if I am lacking in an area of health, wealth, family, relationships, business, sociality, or spirituality. She always reminds me how important it is to celebrate my successes.

Alongside Dr. Pezzini, I have a sort of personal advisory board I go to on different subjects. In addition to paying for my professional life coach, I have a vocal coach for singing, spiritual advisors, specialty business mentors, and a therapist, all of whom I consult with regularly. A key point here is to pay for it – especially with life and business advisors, you get what you pay for, and when you have some skin in the game you value it more. If you are the smartest person in the room, then you're in the wrong room. You are a product of your environment and surrounding yourself with those who you perceive as more intelligent or successful will cause you to strive to be more like them. Swami Paramhansa Yogananda gave us the aphorism, "environment is stronger than will power." The Ramayan scripture states that when you are surrounded with a certain company you will then be like that company. Is your surrounding harvesting your growth?

*See my pictures with Anthony Robbins, teachers featured in The Secret, Sir Richard Branson, Tai Lopez, etc. at www.thepassiveincomebook.com

MY PAST REAL ESTATE SUCCESS STORIES

Fortunately for me, my success story featured on a National Cable & Television broadcast on the Cash Flow Generator infomercial* when I earned a six-figure profit after only my first year in real estate. This, in part, allowed me to jumpstart my success in the real estate industry and eventually at the height of my involvement in the field, I had managed hundreds of tenants across multiple buildings. In the years preceding and following this time, I learned many lessons. The most important ones I learned, though, involved how to compromise and deal with people who weren't always willing to meet in the middle. No matter what field you work in or where you live in the world, you will always come across people who truly believe that they are always right in their opinions or mindsets. Being exposed to this type of personality so early on in my professional life allowed me to use the tactics I gained throughout my property managing days to more efficiently deal with my future bosses, employees, and investors. People-managing skills are amongst the most relevant that you can gain.

Overseeing numerous buildings also meant constantly having to maintain the infrastructure and quality of dwellings. Often enough, a new problem arose – burst pipes, new carpeting needed, leaky ceilings – you name it, I probably dealt with it. These problems had me in consistent contact with contractors, plumbers, electricians, and handymen in general. A majority of the contractors I dealt with were exceedingly unreliable, and this caused me many a setback in getting my apartments move-in-ready. The more time my properties were vacant, the more money I lost. Thankfully I had some financial leeway because of the income my other properties brought in, but for someone with not as many properties, an inefficient contractor could mean the difference between a successful investment in a rental property or a failure. Take your time in choosing whom you work with in maintaining or renovating your building, and always budget for possible money lost if the project takes longer than expected (which it always does).

Unfortunately, alongside difficult tenants and fickle contractors, I also had to deal with lawsuits. Fraud, discrimination in screening applicants, and physical injury on the property are among the most common problems I had to deal with. Fortunately, I ran my properties with the utmost care and honesty, so none of the lawsuits I personally encountered ever succeeded in their intentions. Yet another lesson I can impart upon you relates to that – be honest in your dealings and avoid shortcuts. Even though these things may seem like they provide an immediate benefit, in the long run they are detrimental to your success. In the late 60s, psychologist Walter Mischel led a series of experiments on delayed gratification, which were subsequently named the Stanford Marshmallow Experiments. In these experiments, a young child was given the choice between being able to eat one marshmallow immediately or waiting 10-15 minutes and being able to eat two marshmallows. Decades later, Mischel followed up with the children from the original studies and measured multiple facets of success. Ultimately, the children who were able to delay gratification for a bigger reward down the line were more successful in multiple areas of life, including both professional success and being able to maintain a healthy lifestyle. You can see from this study that success is correlated to one's ability to see into the future and realize that maybe the quickest reward is not the best.

  *See the Infomercial video clip at www.thepassiveincomebook.com

MY PAST INVESTMENT HISTORY

Although investing can have its advantages, it can also be harmful if you aren't careful or attentive with your investments. It also isn't an immediate profit that you earn if you choose to stick with it for the long run, rather than day trading or choosing more short-term investments. Look at the stock market – it varies day-to-day, month-to-month, and year-to-year. Some stocks can increase generously in the matter of weeks while others can take much longer to see the same increase in return. There is no guarantee, either, that you will make money off of your investment, regardless of how accomplished your investment manager is. Companies are unpredictable, as there are so many things that can contribute to their value, and sometimes despite your best efforts and time spent researching, an investment can go the opposite way intended.

A few companies that I invested in ultimately ended up shutting down before I could cash out my funds, and I had to quickly rebalance my finances when faced with these unexpected losses. These setbacks taught me to more carefully weigh the risks and benefits of the investment portfolios I considered, even if it took up a little more of my time than I intended. I viewed these losses as obstacles I had to overcome and didn't let them discourage me from future investments, if a seemingly profitable one came across my path.

Another business venture that aided in my financial success was my involvement in network marketing businesses, also known as multi-level marketing. You've probably heard of a few of these – Amway is one of the better-known network marketing businesses I was heavily involved in, as well as Prepaid Legal Services (now called Legal Shield), and Javita. The basic idea of these types of companies is that an individual buys in to the company and can earn commission on the products that they end up selling. This type of "employment" allows you to be flexible in your hours, work from home, and essentially be your own boss. They typically require a minimal initial investment to get a sample of the product you're selling and to gain a feel for how to market it when you start selling to other people. This type of business venture usually attracts people who are looking for flexible employment and if you can dedicate enough time and effort, it can end up being quite the lucrative option. The personal development and leadership ability gained here in their proven system are priceless.

My father would say to me that you should have 3 types of people in your life: 1) someone greater than you to learn from, 2) someone at your level to exchange ideas with, and 3) someone younger than you to teach what you've learned. Network Marketing provides an opportunity for all 3 with your up-line, down-line, and sideline people.

DISCOVER YOUR PASSION

An easy way to discover what you're truly passionate about is to take a step back and look at your hobbies. Hobbies are what you choose to do in your free time and are things you genuinely enjoy, rather than being something you feel obligated to do because it provides for your family or allows you to lead an extravagant lifestyle. You will be most successful in endeavors that you're passionate about since working towards your goals won't seem like work.

Unfortunately, sometimes your hobbies don't necessarily match up with what kind of income you need in life. That's when you try your best to find a career field that you can be successful in, while also making time to do the things you truly enjoy. Maintaining a consistent effort towards having one or two interests outside of work will help keep you feeling satisfied with where you are in life.

Another way to work towards becoming the most successful person you can be is looking at why you do the things you do. I've noticed throughout my life that as long as you're doing something for the right reasons, things will generally fall in your favor. Why you're doing something ultimately determines how you do it. If you start something with good intentions, you will put in the effort necessary for making sure your goals come to fruition. On the other hand, if you work towards something but with the wrong intentions, you may still become successful, although there is a smaller chance of that and your achievements may not feel as satisfying as if why you did that was for a purer reason. This is yet another reason why you should look at your hobbies and try your hardest to find a career that matches up with them. If what you end up doing for the rest of your life is something you're truly passionate about, then you will have become the most successful person you can be.

For me, my passions have to do mainly with the arts and performing in front of an audience of thousands of people locally and internationally. My favorite quote is from the movie Braveheart "Everyone dies, but not everyone truly lives." I feel truly alive when I sing with my band on stage, act on stage for charity, emcee events, and even do TV/Radio interviews. All of these were done alongside my investments in the stock market, FOREX market, and real estate, and they helped me maintain a feeling of being creative, something I truly cherish. Even though I didn't make a full-time career out of any of my hobbies, I was still able to pursue them because I found a way to run my business efficiently and have enough free time. Without a way to express my creative side, I most likely would have failed at most of the goals I tried to achieve career-wise as I would have felt confined in a world where I wasn't able to be completely myself.

I also derive satisfaction from contributing back to my community or the world I live in through charity work. To some people this can mean writing a check for some non-profit organization, while for others it can mean being directly involved with the charity through volunteering or being on the board. Some have the time for the latter while for most all they can contribute is a small monetary donation. I love the Sai Baba quote that says "Hands that serve mankind are holier than lips that pray". I find as long as I'm able to lend a helping hand in some way, I feel as if I've done some good with my life. However, I do advise you take caution with the charities you choose to invest in, as some don't actually give back as much as the general public thinks they do.

Luckily enough for me, even though it may have happened upon me later in life than I preferred, I found something I was genuinely passionate about that I could also make money off of. That was investing on a diverse scale. I loved the continual education that was required of investing. I always had to know what was going on in the market or in foreign economies so that I could try and predict which of my investments was going to become profitable, or which ones I should just cut my losses with. I then started hiring people smarter than me. I ended up loving it so much that I chose to start my own private investment club and became the go-to guy for people that wanted ideas about passive income investing. I have faith and hope that everyone in life will eventually be able to find an opportunity to be successful and happy like I have, even if it may cross your path when you least expect it.

PASSIVE INCOME

Passive income is part of the idea of unearned income; essentially, it is income that is received on a consistent basis with minimal effort put in to manage and maintain it. You can receive unearned or passive income from things such as pensions, inheritance, and property income, which don't require any active effort to profit from. These types of earnings are what people typically become wealthy from, rather than the salary they earn from their day jobs. Instead of living directly off of their earnings from their day jobs, many people can cut down on their daily expenses and use those savings to invest in opportunities that allow them to earn a passive income.

The most common ways to earn passive income are through rental and investment income. Rental income initially is not purely passive income, as the initial down payment and maintenance of the property can require a lot of time and effort depending on the state and quality of the building or buildings you choose to purchase. Even after this initial investment, there is still a consistent effort that needs to be put in for rental properties to maintain profitability. You have to collect checks from every tenant each month (which may not always go through) and deal with a multitude of problems that arise from difficult tenants or neighbors, or even from the infrastructure of the building itself. Rental income, however, is more a passive income than your day job, and can sometimes even be more profitable if managed in an efficient way.

In contrast, investment income is on the opposite spectrum of passive income and requires little effort after the initial investment to start earning profit. However, sometimes investing necessitates quite a large chunk of money to begin earning even a small percentage of gain. Looking at just profiting from dividends, which are payments made by a corporation to its shareholders, to make even $1,000 a year with a 4% annual dividend payout (a pretty hefty payout) you have to invest $25,000. In cases like these, it's best to do your research beforehand and find which companies are slotted to be the most profitable in the next year, as they use a fraction of their retained earnings as dividends to shareholders. The more profit a company earns, the more it can pay out to its shareholders.

There are other ways you can earn passive income through investing, too. You can trade commodities, stocks, currencies on the foreign exchange market (FOREX), securities, and even precious metals. I hire FOREX traders who I know that leverage my time so that I don't have to trade myself, or monitor the global news reports constantly. Each of these options has their advantages and drawbacks, but they are all considered a type of passive income. One of the more frequently chosen of the aforementioned options is investing in a mutual fund, which is professionally managed and pools money from multiple investors to purchase securities. This type of investment is most useful in planning for retirement, as it has a decreased amount of risk compared to investing in individual securities since a fund typically holds a diverse portfolio of securities. If one of the securities in the fund doesn't do well, chances are at least a few others did well enough to make up for the loss attributable to that one security. However, mutual funds come with fees when you buy and sell shares and are already "pre-packaged." This means you don't have as much freedom to customize your investment portfolio as you would have investing in individual securities yourself.

Another way I have found to earn passive income is through tax lien certificates. A lien is a type of security over a property to ensure that the owner pays back any debt or obligation they owe to the lien holder. A tax lien certificate, specifically, is for when a property has a lien placed upon it due to unpaid property taxes. They ultimately represent the right to foreclose on a property when there is failure of property tax payments. These certificates can be auctioned off to investors, who pay the amount of taxes owed on the property in order to then gain the right to collect the unpaid taxes from the owners plus the current rate of interest on tax lien certificates. These rates can range anywhere from 5 to 36 percent and the property owner has a period of 6 months to 3 years to pay back the taxes and interest. If the owner fails to do so by the end of the redemption period, then the lien holder is allowed to start foreclosure proceedings and take ownership of the property. Either way, with careful consideration of which tax lien certificates you choose to buy, you could earn a fair amount of passive income. However, you must figure out what your responsibilities are concerning obtaining ownership of the lien – in some states, you are required to send multiple letters at different time points notifying the owners that you now own the lien and if they fail to repay their taxes, you can foreclose on their property. Some even have expiration dates where if you don't initiate foreclosure proceedings within a certain time after the redemption period, you no longer have the right to the property. All in all, tax lien certificates have the potential to be highly profitable if you can do the research required of them.

A less well-known method of generating passive income is through owning or leasing ATM machines. The way to make a passive income through this is with the service fee that most ATMs impose upon the user. Typically, these range anywhere from $2-$5 and with each transaction on the machine, that is what you end up earning. Although it may seem like a miniscule amount at first glance, imagine if just 10 people a day used your machine. At the low end of service fees, that still equates to $600 a month with you essentially doing nothing. First off, you have to make the decision to either purchase or lease an ATM machine. Even though purchasing an ATM requires a larger initial investment, it is ultimately less expensive than leasing a machine, as you own it outright rather than having to pay a monthly fee to use and profit from it. There are some legal hoops that you may have to jump through, though, such as registering the ATM machine with your county clerk if you plan on running it under a business' name. After you ensure you have all the proper licenses, you can start placing the ATM machines in carefully picked locations, which is ultimately what matters most when trying to profit from this type of venture. You want to guarantee that your ATM is placed in an area that receives enough foot traffic and is far away enough from a bank that it is more convenient for people to withdraw money from your ATM than the bank.

Finally, the last approach I'll mention here to generating passive income that I have personally done and can suggest is through product sourcing or drop shipping. Product sourcing is a way to sell items on eBay or Amazon where the sellers never actually handle the item and instead it is sent directly from the warehouse to the buyer. The sellers of the products purchase in bulk from the warehouse, but the warehouse holds the items for the seller and then ships it out when a buyer purchases a unit. By buying in bulk, the seller is able to receive a discount on the item, which they can then choose to sell full price to the buyer. This is essentially where your profit comes from through product sourcing. There are some disadvantages to this method though – most notably is the fact that drop shippers frequently run out of stock of their more popular items, which the seller doesn't find out until after they sell the item and notify the supplier that it needs to be shipped. This results in bad feedback for your store on eBay, and can decrease the amount of traffic you end up getting. In addition, there has recently been a rise in drop shippers exporting directly from China – essentially drop shippers are now directly selling their product on eBay themselves. This is a difficult market to enter specifically on eBay, as shoppers on this website are typically looking to strike a bargain, while you're looking to make a profit. Furthermore, some suppliers don't offer the true wholesale price on their products when you're buying on the minimum side of a bulk order. However, if you're able to establish a satisfying professional relationship with your drop shipper, and ensure that you're getting a real wholesale price, then this type of venture could be profitable.

PRIVATE INVESTMENT CLUBS

In order to benefit my friends, family, and business partners as much as possible, I started a private investment club to educate them using the experience I've gained in over the past decade. The diversity of ventures I've pursued and achieved success in makes me a unique and extensive expert on passive income. Through all of my trials and errors, I've finally figured out ways to make money work for me, rather than me working for money. I want to be able to share that knowledge with as many people as possible, which is why I decided to write this book.

If you are an accredited investor or a sophisticated investor and get accepted into a private investment club, it truly can be a passive investment – you don't need to work to earn any profit. On my website, www.thepassiveincomebook. com, you can read testimonials and referrals from multiple different people who have chosen to learn smart investing ideas and strategies with me. Like me, they're able to spend less time trying to earn money and worrying about it, and more time living a passion-filled life.

Additionally, I work with a group of commercial investors that invest in multi-family apartment building units in emerging markets and help people get a higher than average rate of return secured by real estate in the USA. I've learned about this type of commercial investing directly from Real Estate Guru David Lindahl and his mentorship program. There are so many cash flow and equity position opportunities available to someone as a private lender. Private loans can be loaned to a real estate investor and secured by real estate for rehabilitation projects, flips, or rental holdings. Private loan investors are given a first, or a second mortgage, that secures their legal interest in the property and secures their investment. "Secured" means that their money is secured by an asset, which in this case is the real estate property.

Many people don't realize that they can even invest their retirement income into real estate and other investments themselves, tax-free. You can roll it over and not get charged any penalties with a self-directed IRA. This can be an incredible way to leave a legacy for generational wealth.

RISKS, CAUTION, AND SAFETY

Like with any new adventure, there is inherent risk in investing your money in the ways I've previously mentioned. With investing, there are two basic types of risk – systematic and unsystematic. Systematic is a type of risk that you are unable to avoid when investing and it can affect a broad spectrum of assets. A good example of a systematic risk would be an important political event that could possibly influence the entire market. On the other hand, unsystematic risk, or specific risk, only affects a small number of assets. For example, if union workers from the port were to strike, then only stocks for companies that dealt with that port would be affected. Thankfully though, unlike systematic risk, you can protect yourself from unsystematic risk through diversification. The more diverse an investment portfolio you have, the more you can ensure that a drop in one stock doesn't equate to a drop in your entire portfolio, since you have different kinds of stocks that can make up for that loss. However, there is a tradeoff between risk and return – higher risk stocks typically have a higher payout while lower risk stocks tend to have a lower return. This is where you have to ask yourself, how much are you willing to gamble? Do you have the freedom to take a loss or are you still too early on in your financial journey to afford that potential loss? I want you to use the lessons from this book to be able to get yourself to a point where you feel comfortable occasionally taking those risks to get a higher payout. As long as you don't continuously invest in high-risk stocks or securities and make smart investments, you could have the opportunity to receive a high return.

I do want to caution you though. No matter how much you diversify your portfolio, the risk of investing will never be zero. You can, however, reduce it as much as possible through diversification. This doesn't just mean making sure to invest in different types of companies, but also different types of investment vehicles. There are stocks, mutual funds, real estate, foreign currency, and bonds, among other things. Choosing multiple vehicles across various industries ensures that if one takes a dive, it's more than likely that your other investments are safe and sound. A not well-known way to diversify your portfolio to reduce risk is to also vary the risk of your investments. To minimize risk, you don't have to commit yourself to only choosing blue chip stocks or other types of vehicles with very low risk. If you pick investments with varying rates of return, you can help guarantee that a high return will make up for any losses in other industries or vehicles.

If you feel like you don't have enough free time to initially commit to diversifying your own portfolio, you can always trust a professional to cultivate your portfolio for you, or invest your money in an already-created and vetted portfolio. This chapter has been all about how to make money work for you so that you have financial freedom, and as I said before, a good way to start is to delegate and get educated. So why don't you take that next step? Start investing and share with me your personal success stories and breakthroughs. Contact us today to learn more about our informational products and seminars.

To read more about K. Raj Singh's experiences and wisdom, get his newest book titled "Control $, Before $ Controls You: Finding Your Passion Through Passive Income" and visit www.thepassiveincomebook.com

Outshine the Competition:
Coming Out on Top in the Interview Process

OSSY BOTHA

"Sometimes one creates a dynamic impression by saying something, and sometimes one creates as significant an impression by remaining silent."

– The Dalai Lama

Interview Dynamics introduces a concept which helps Career & Job Seekers prepare, refine and polish the "how & what" in any interview situation; how to describe and what to say about their skills and experiences. - Ossy

There are no two ways about it. Job-hunting in today's harsh economic realities is tougher than ever before. If the prospect of job interviews sends shivers up and down your spine, you're not alone. Global expansion and outsourcing, technological innovation and a spate of economic crises have changed the employment landscape beyond recognition, and a job-seeker is stepping into an unknown that few have wandered into before. In short, nailing the interview is much more of a priority than ever before.

There are new rules when it comes to looking for a job, and it's no longer just about possessing the right resumé. Whether you are fresh out of college, changing careers or wanting a promotion in your current company or current field, you have to go through an interview, come across as a credible candidate, and then show you are the best fit for the job. You have to deliver a flawless performance while juggling the stresses of applying for several jobs at the same time. It's a tremendous burden to bear, and it's no surprise that many applicants cringe at the thought of readying themselves for an interview. There are loads of how-to books on the shelves in bookstores and libraries, many of them filled with theory, tips and advice -- none of which you'll remember in the heat of an interview.

So, how do you really get up to speed to out-prepare and outshine the competition? The solution is quite simple. We help you gain the confidence and the assuredness you need so that, rather than stepping into the interview with clammy palms and nervous tics, you'll breeze in with a confident stride, a smile on your face and a strong handshake, and come out a winner.

WHAT IS INTERVIEW DYNAMICS AND ITS PURPOSE?

Each one of us performs various roles in our lives. You are a brother, son, boyfriend, colleague, uncle, husband or a mother, daughter, BFF, stepsister, aunt and so on. You take on the roles that are expected of you without question and switch from being parent to sibling in the blink of an eye.

Similarly, as a work colleague we take on our different profiles while we perform the various roles applicable to our job criteria, whether we are the Office Cleaner or the CEO.

In the office, you are a colleague and, simultaneously, a department head. You have to report to a board of several bosses and, at the same time, have to take care of several junior employees. You have to motivate the ranks below you, you have to sell new ideas to your bosses and you have to take care of all the paperwork! Basically, you wear several hats at work and, during the course of a workday, you move seamlessly from one role to another.

In Interview Dynamics, we help you to do the same. We teach you to think of yourself as a business, and we remove the personal ego from the preparation. The brutal truth is that, no matter how qualified you may be, there is always the possibility of someone more highly skilled than yourself. You can bone up as much as you can by reading books on interviewing, rehearsing your answers and doing your homework, but it's how you fare during your interview that seals your fate.

So, rather than have you present yourself as a nervous candidate, we take you step-by-step through the practicalities of preparing for an interview. We guide you through several processes and we help you change your mindset. There are many books on interviewing skills and they advocate that you brush up on your strengths and weaknesses, but do they tell you how to do just that?

When I was coaching a client through Interview Dynamics, I asked her to tell me about a mistake she had made at work. She was totally flabbergasted by the question and several awkward minutes ticked by and she still couldn't come up with an answer. Luckily, this was a practice run, and she subsequently used the tools in Interview Dynamics to prepare herself for the real thing.

We build your confidence through shifting your perspective in order to tap the infinite resources that already reside within you and to leverage the skills inherent in you to suit the occasion. The simple truth is that you are a multi-talented person and, rather than presenting yourself as a one-dimensional candidate to the employer, how about viewing yourself as a business which we call Firm You (Pty) Ltd?

This company, Firm You, has a range of services and products, namely your work experience, credentials and other qualities such as leadership, communication and motivational skills that will greatly benefit the end-consumer of the company you are interviewing with. In return for supplying these "goods and services", you are paid money, as you would in any business transaction, in the form of a salary.

Residing within you, waiting to be called to the fore, are several important figures of authority in the business – the Managing Director, the Financial Director, the Sales Director and the Project Director. Depending on the task at hand during the interview, you will wear the hat that most suits the role you are playing. For example, during that phase of interview when you have to persuade the (slightly skeptical) interviewer that you're the best person for the job, you bring forth the Sales Director of Firm You, because he or she is the best suited for this particular task.

Let's take a pause and try this idea on for size. Let's pretend that you are the Sales Director of a very successful company named Firm You. You're present at a meeting selling a business or service. You are not a single person. Instead, you are a business that contains a multitude of talents, skills and viewpoints.

Can you see how this change in perspective takes the sting of anxiety and stress out of the interviewing process? Can you feel the shift that takes place within when you re-imagine the process as a sales meeting, not a nerve-wracking interview? That, in simple terms, is the essence of Interview Dynamics.

We take you through various exercises that are the cornerstones of Interview Dynamics. Each of them is meant to prepare you so thoroughly that you'll be ready with an answer to any question that is thrown at you during the interview. The cornerstones of Interview Dynamics are: -

1. Knowing yourself

2. Projecting yourself with confidence and communicating with clarity

3. The Business Plan

We briefly mentioned the various figures of authority within Firm You; now let's take a closer look at what each of them encompasses before explaining how they kick in during the interview process.

THE ASSETS THAT LIE WITHIN

To recap, Firm You (Pty) Ltd is You. The company you are hoping to land a job in is a potential customer called the Prospective Employer.

There are four important job designations within Firm You: -

1. Managing Director – The MD is the visionary who, through investment in education, training and work experience, has guided Firm You to

where it is today. As MD, he or she wants to direct the business to the next level.

2. Financial Director – He or she knows the value of your business (or your salary) and must have this figure at his or her fingertips in order to arrive at a fair deal during negotiations with the prospective employer.

3. Sales Director – The Sales Director is always on the ball. For the Sales Director, an interview is just another business meeting. He or she is the public face of Firm You, and is always "selling" on the job during the daily course of work. Let's not mistake "selling" with just being words and fluff and little else. Firm You has to back up the sales pitch of the Sales Director with a solid, outstanding performance.

4. Project Director - He or she is the one who goes all out into doing the research and the homework. The Project Director delves into the ins and outs of a potential job – analyzing the job description, the tasks and projects that make up the job, the skills, training and education required – all with the goal of matching your assets and qualifications to the job description. By verifying all that is required for the position, you can clearly show how you are able to deliver.

BUILDING THE BUSINESS OF FIRM YOU

We start with you wearing the hat of a Project Director who, in a manner of speaking, has to draft out a blueprint for a major project. Imagine a project director tasked with bidding for a project to build a bridge. He or she has to identify the assets and resources available, pinpoint strengths, weaknesses and experience of such resources, organize them into various functional teams, identify key tasks and lay out a timeline.

In this case, you're the Project Director and Firm You is your task at hand. There are three steps that you have to undertake:

- Task A: Brainstorm and jot down all your skills, experiences, extra training, your problem-solving expertise, and strengths and weaknesses relevant to the position you are applying for. This is a no-holds barred session; let go, write down everything that comes to mind. Don't edit yourself -- that comes later. At this stage, use as many pages as you need.

- Task B: Organize the mass of information from Task A into distinct categories relevant to the functions in the job description. Categories include education, skills, competencies, tasks, projects, jobs functions and so forth. This continues until all information from Task A has been neatly slotted under the various appropriate headings.

- Task C: Chunk up information from Task 2 and extract only key tasks appropriate to each heading. This is the final step in your homework as Project Director. You take only the most relevant information from each of the categories in Task B and transfer them to another page with the following important headings: education, courses, tech-skills, job functions, strengths and weaknesses, salary, questions about the job. Think of this as the final step in connecting the dots between what you have and what is required.

KNOW YOURSELF:
COMMUNICATION + CLARIFICATION + COMMUNICATION

These next exercises are to get you to thoroughly know yourself. By working through the three tasks from A to C, you are building and re-familiarizing yourself with a database of resources, competencies and skills that you already have at your disposal. Through this exercise, you'll regain confidence in who you really are and refresh your memory as to your creativity, achievements and accomplishments.

During the interview, you'll be wearing the hat of the Sales Director, who is out to sell the business of Firm You (Pty) Ltd. Having done this kind of homework, you'll be able to answer difficult and awkward questions with credibility and authority, and basically demonstrate that you have all it takes to land the job.

Having all the important bits of information at your fingertips because of the hard work put into preparation, you, as the Sales Director, are able to communicate clearly.

You will also be in a position of strength to answer with clarity, without hemming or hawing or taking awkward pauses, any questions the interviewer may ask of you.

Lastly, you will come across as a confident figure because you are well-prepared; you are able to adroitly handle any awkward questions thrown at you on any aspect of the job at hand.

REMUNERATION

You have come this far in the interview process, and now you could come undone in what is inevitably a sticky issue: how much you should be paid. No matter how well you have performed so far, this issue could be the deal-breaker if you don't put sufficient thought into your worth.

In Interview Dynamics, we provide a different take on this subject. We give you a formula, one coined by your Financial Director (it's now his or her time to step up to the plate), so you can reframe the salary negotiation not as a do-or-die situation, but as a means of getting a fair return on your output.

When you think about it, you strike a deal with someone who sells you a product or service because you think and feel you're getting a fair return on your money. Let's take this point a little further. Your Prospective Employer buys from Firm You and pays you in the form of your salary (Total Cost to Company or TCTC), in order to get desirable products and services to sell to his end customer in return for money. Naturally, he will want to make a profit on top of this cost. In order for the Prospective Employer to make a fair return and to strike a deal with you, your Financial Director values Firm You as follows: -

TCTC X 4 = Your Salary X 1 + TCTC X 3 =
Profit to Prospective Employer = Fair Deal.

FROM PREP TO THE DOTTED LINE: SO WHO ARE YOU?

Now that we've covered the groundwork, there's still a little way to go before you get to sign on the dotted line. You have to be comfortable talking about yourself and polishing your storytelling skills. The more success stories you can offer, the better you show yourself as being likely to achieve equivalent success in the future. You have to be able to talk about yourself because, without fail, the question will come up "Tell us about yourself." You're certainly not boosting your hiring chances if you hesitate or respond with something unprofessional like "What do you wish to know?"

With that in mind, you have to be fully prepared to talk in detail about work that you have done in the past that made a difference to your then employer. As part of our process in Interview Dynamics, we'll guide you to coming up with concrete examples such as how you successfully closed a sale with an important customer or how you found solutions to an ongoing and expensive problem. Be conversant with your strengths and weaknesses to help your interviewer connect the dots as to why you are a winning pick for the job. This phase of the process is not as tough as it sounds because of all the prep work previously done by your Project Director.

Being asked about your mistakes is a normal thing. Do not panic, because it is in fact something that you can prepare for. Take the time right now to consider what you have done wrong. As you talk about the incident, talk about how you fixed it, how you learned from it, and how you would prevent something like that from ever happening again! This shows initiative, and it also gives your Prospective Employer an idea of how you could solve any of their problems in the future.

THE BUSINESS PLAN

Now, you turn the spotlight on the job itself. Is this project worth bidding for, so to speak? Does the job in question meet your needs? In a manner of speaking, Firm You has to analyze this opportunity, just as any business considering a potential investment would, and thus come up with a business plan. As Project Director, you have done the research and crunched the analytics. The Managing Director then weighs up whether or not this new job will take Firm You and its profitability to the next level. The Financial Director suggests the price that Firm You wants and, if everyone is in agreement, it is then up to the Sales Director to sell Firm You.

QUESTIONING THE QUESTIONER

As the interview process winds down, you may feel that you are in the home stretch. However, there is still the area where you are allowed to ask the person giving the interview any questions you have in mind. Make no mistake about it -- this is as much a test as anything else that has transpired before.

In the previous part of the interview, you were being tested to see how well you responded to stimuli. Now you are being judged on how well you are able to act independently.

Remember that, if you have done your research about the company and have the business plan at hand, you have plenty to talk about. For example, if you have noticed that the company has been very active on social media, mention it and ask if there are responsibilities, considering your ease at social marketing, which you can cover. This shows initiative, and it also allows the questioner to see how interested you are in the job.

You may choose to ask what they feel the biggest challenge of the job will be. Not only will this give you some very important information about the job, you'll also discover that it gives you a chance to tell them how you would deal with it.

Do not allow the space in the interview where you are allowed to ask questions catch you by surprise. They are watching for that because this is where many people show how unprepared or unsuitable they are. For example, if you are interviewing at a non-profit organisation and, suddenly, all you can talk about are vacation days, there's likely a mismatch there!

Do not miss out on this great opportunity to show your prospective employers how interested you are in what they do. This isn't a time when the tables are turned. In fact, it is just a shift in the form of the interview. They are still looking at you, and you still need to impress them!

FINALIZING THE INTERVIEW DYNAMICS PROCESS

Reading is all well and good, but now you need to put some physical effort into the process. With all of this preparation, which is integral throughout Interview Dynamics, you have all the raw information that you need to make a great impression at your interview. Now you need to refine it, and that starts with writing.

Whether you are most comfortable with a pen and pencil, or you are someone who is most at ease in front of a computer screen, you are now going to sit down and put your interviewing skills and writing skills to work.

Sit down, clear your head and start typing up the interview as you imagine it happening to you. Write out all of the questions that you think will be asked, and spend some time with each one. What do you think they are asking you, and what do you think they are looking for? Then, using this information, craft your responses.

Some people balk at writing line-by- line responses. They fear that it will feel rehearsed or simply trite, but the truth of the matter is that it is not as though you will be reading these things out loud to the person who is interviewing you! Instead, writing out your response will give you a strong foundation on which you can build your answers. You will know the content of what you want to say, but as the situation develops and as you gain more confidence and more mastery over what is going on, you will simply be using the original groundwork as a springboard to the right answer.

When you are preparing to sell yourself to a prospective buyer, you will find that one of the most important things that you can do is to be prepared. Once you have the information that you need, go over it again and again until you know it completely. You may think that you know your strengths and your weaknesses but, until you have been over them a few times, you will never be able to explain them to others.

Good preparation is the key to success and, not only must you have the abilities that the employer is asking for, you must also be someone who can talk about them and who can make the employer understand what you are offering. Do not fall behind simply because, after all the preparation you have done, you fall down on the delivery!

A PROFESSIONAL APPLICATION

It can often feel as if you are walking a fine line between presenting yourself as a unique individual and standing out for being too silly or too personal but, with Interview Dynamics, we show you how to walk that line with absolutely no fear at all. When you think about the fact that there may be dozens, perhaps even hundreds or thousands, of people applying for the job that you want, it is natural to get cold feet but, by applying the principles of Interview Dynamics, you have the advantage of a strong foundation to fall back on.

We show you how to create a rock-solid presentation for your application, and it is founded upon sheer professionalism. A resumé and an application get your foot in the door at the place where you want to work, but being able to demonstrate that you have a lot to bring to the table and that you have what it takes will send your name right to the top of the candidate list.

The key is to leave your ego out of it. You have done many things in your life, and you have certainly done things to be proud of. You have conquered mountains and of course you are proud of the effort that you have put in. However, the thing to remember is that the business that is speaking to you is not interested as much in how hard you work, but in seeing the results that you produce.

This is the key to professionalism and one that few people really grasp. In the quest to learn more about the business that you want to work with, get to know them. What results are they looking for? Do they want their company name to be known as a leader in green initiatives? Are they looking to make sure that they always come out on top in their field? Are they hoping to reform an image that might have been tarnished or dented in recent years?

If you want to make your application stand out, remember that it is less about you and more about the people with whom you are trying to communicate. There has never been a better time to be you, and you must show the company that you are considering why that might be.

Leave your ego at the door, and remember that your application needs to show them why they not only want you, but why they need you!

TAKING SCORE AND PRESENTING THE SALES PITCH

We are now almost at the end of the process. Just to make sure all your bases are covered, we'll score all the prep work you have done to identify what may be missing and what may need to be further supplemented. Once you're satisfied with the score, we'll move on to the last section.

As the final step, we'll run you through a self-interview where you ask questions of yourself and write down your answers to take a measure of how effectively your Sales Director is pitching your business. Are you selling your business in an efficient and professional manner? Where do you need to be refined and polished? What more do you need to know? Are you fully prepared to proceed and come through with flying colors?

By presenting yourself as a business, you are in fact able to distance yourself from the personal anxieties and insecurities that often dog an interview. Instead, you are selling a business you believe in – Firm You – and by doing so you are separating yourself from the sea of applicants and showing up as a winner!

There are multiple uses of Interview Dynamics. It is not just a process to get a new job. You can use all the steps embodied in Interview Dynamics to perform a self-assessment of your work before your annual review or, if you are lobbying for a promotion, use this same process to clearly establish why you deserve better, what additional skills and competencies you have to offer, how you have sought to improve yourself throughout the year, and how the company is going to get a fair value for your services. This process works for anyone, whether you are reporting to the financial director who answers to the board of directors or whether you are an office clerk reporting to the office manager.

Remember, you may not always be the best candidate with the most premium skills. But if you come across as being fully prepared and fully confident, you will be the most memorable and very likely the most winning candidate.

I wish you every success in selling Firm You (Pty) Ltd.

Hi, my name is Ossy Botha. I am from Johannesburg South Africa where I've worked in the recruitment industry for 32 years and counting.

Over this period of time, I have recruited and placed people in various positions and in many different companies – both large and small.

The positions which I recruit for cover a wide range of disciplines -- from senior management level to office support, administration, sales, logistics, production, technical support personnel and the like.

In a nutshell, from the front door receptionist to the back door of the business and from the bottom to the top floor.

Throughout the years, I have attended many courses, read articles on interviewing skills and gained interview techniques from the internet, all of which have proven to be very helpful.

The Interview Dynamics concept is vastly different from any existing techniques. In fact, I have not come across any material that remotely resembles what Interview Dynamics has to offer.

The reason for incorporating Interview Dynamics into your preparation is that it is a deep and thorough process during which you really get to know yourself while gaining tools and skills on how to represent yourself during an interview.

Interview Dynamics changes your perception from an applicant hoping to land the job, to that of a Company Director attending a business meeting.

Over the past years I have interviewed a countless number of people with whom I have shared the Interview Dynamics concept, all of whom have been grateful for receiving this methodology.

Therefore, I would like to share this accolade received from Savashni who was applying for a local and overseas creditor's administrator position. After our initial discussion, I walked her through the Interview Dynamics methodology.

Unfortunately, she was not invited to the prospective employer for an interview because they had just offered the opportunity to another applicant whom I had introduced to the company simply because she could begin work immediately.

However, Savashni continued to use Interview Dynamics to prepare for other job interviews as she was fully committed to the process. This is what she has to say:

"I met with Ossy in January 2014 for a position advertised for a certain company. Unfortunately I did not manage to secure an interview, but the effect of my meeting with Ossy did not end there.

I have since been to various agencies and interviews and, as of last week, I was successful in securing three jobs -- all finance related, at three different companies. That was such a surprise, from having no interviews to securing three jobs. Based on my career path, I chose the first company and will be starting with them in the 2nd week of April.

All of this was possible because I used the tips and advice I received from Ossy. I used his techniques and focused on my key achievements and abilities and put myself forward to each of my interviewers as a business, not just as an individual. His techniques really helped me to build my self-confidence.

My meeting with Ossy was really a life lesson that I shall take with me into my future. I honestly don't believe that I would have been so successful in all three interviews if I did not use Ossy's Interview Dynamic techniques.

Thank you very much. I wish Ossy and the business everything of the best for the future.

Kind Regards,
Savashni"

Should you be interested in obtaining these techniques, log onto **www.jobmasters.co.za**

Change your world. Don't miss out on achieving your career goals due to poor interviewing skills.

Thank you for reading my version of how to prepare for your forthcoming interview. The effort that you put into this concept will improve your chances of taking your business to the next level.

Motivation Does Activate and Sustain Behaviour

How to Bring Results in Life and Business

JULIE HOGBIN

B efore we talk about motivation in any great detail, it would be a good idea to cover the basics about what motivation really is. There are many, many, theories and huge amounts of research has been conducted on the subject over many decades. To be honest, with all the information out there it can be confusing as to what it all means.

One thing is for sure, one theory — one piece of information — does not cover it all as each researcher has their own bent and interpretation on the subject. It is when you are able to link it all together that it starts to make sense and you are able to do something with the information to help yourself.

I have researched, read about, practiced, and taught this subject to over 20,000 Leaders in Life, Business and the Entrepreneur market, both one-on-one and in small groups for very nearly three decades, and I am still learning.

This chapter is based around my knowledge, my interpretation, and a definition of Motivation that I have worked with for a long time. I have neither found nor developed a better definition — yet!

"Motivation is a conscious or unconscious driving force that arouses and directs action towards the achievement of a desired goal."

ClaimYourDestiny.global   #ConsciousLeadership

So, what does this mean in reality? It means that we are motivated by internal and external factors and that sometimes we know what those factors are and sometimes we don't: Our actions and thoughts are both conscious and unconscious in nature. It also means that the motives provoke a reaction and an action that help us 'get' something we want — a goal — and as a driving force they are powerful.

So my 1st questions to you are:

- What is your goal?

- What are you working towards?

- How many goals do you have?

- What is driving you?

- How conscious are you?

Motivation is an internal force; we are the only ones who can motivate us. Motivation can be affected by external influences. Ultimately it is us, and only us, that make the decision to do or not to do something. Nobody can make you feel or do anything! It is your absolute choice to capitulate and do, or to resist and not do.

We make the decision based on the information we have at the time and how confident we feel. There are many emotions and personal characteristics that come into play when we are talking about motivation and all that entails.

When we say that others motivate us what it really means is that they have created an environment that inspires us to do something. We make the decision out of fear in some cases, because we know it makes sense in other cases, because we aspire to be like the individual, or, more simply, just because we want to.

For you, and everybody else, your desired goal always provides you with a positive outcome. It gives you something you want even if that want is unconsciously driven. For others viewing it from their perspective, that outcome may be viewed as negative.

Let me explain what I mean with a couple of examples.

Addicts of any description do whatever it takes to fuel their need. They are achieving their desired outcome with more alcohol, more food, less food, more drugs, or just more of something, and they will go to extreme lengths to get it, such as selling personal and other people's belongings, lying and deceiving, going into debt and stealing.

Someone comes home with great intent of doing some research, maybe to write a book or to do some personal development such as going to the gym, and they end up sitting in front of the TV for hours with a bottle of wine. What is their driving force? We may not understand it as the viewer but there is definitely one for the person being observed.

Let's look at a couple of positive examples with a more generally accepted encouraging outcome.

A young person decides what they want to achieve in their life. They study like crazy to get the grades required to get to the top university and to study in a class of four with the top professor in their subject matter field, and they achieve it.

An individual from an underprivileged background wants to change their life, achieve greater things than have ever been achieved in their family, and become independently wealthy, and they are successful in achieving their goals.

Now for every example shared the opposite can be true as well. Not everybody becomes an addict, not everyone slouches in front of the TV, not every student achieves their potential, and not every underprivileged individual becomes independently wealthy.

"Everything you do is goal-driven. Everything you do is because you want the end result — whatever that end result may be!"

ClaimYourDestiny.global   #ConsciousLeadership

The examples are all based on how motivated the individual is to achieve their goal. Now if you know your goal consciously, can keep it in focus and resist the temptation of your old ways, you can achieve marvellous results.

The rest of this chapter will look at what drives you and how you can change your habits and behaviours over a period both short and long term, with the aim to achieve whatever it is you want.

I reference no theory in this chapter. There are many to read and learn which are of use to us all intellectually and unless the theory is practically applied and interpreted into reality all they remain are theories. I have spent decades interpreting theories into real life behaviours that make a difference for the better.

A few more questions for you to think about first.

- What are your drivers?

- What are your values?

- What is your risk tolerance?

- How much do you want to fit in with the 'norm' of your social group?

- How much do you really want, on a scale of 1 to 10, the thing it is you are aiming to achieve?

- How comfortable are you with change?

There are a lot more questions to ask but these will start you on the journey to understand your own motivators.

"Your motives create your habits, for good and bad, as they are your driving force."

ClaimYourDestiny.global   #ConsciousLeadership

There is so much information coming at us on a minute by minute basis.

We make thousands upon thousands of decisions every day — so many in fact, we cannot be conscious of all the decisions, to do or not to do something, that we do make. We would be completely overwhelmed if we did.

So what do we do? We create patterns of behaviour that we do not have to think about, as it is quicker that way, to achieve our outcomes. We create habits that get us what we want in the easiest manner.

"Your habits have created your behaviour through your values, beliefs, and attitudes."

ClaimYourDestiny.global   #ConsciousLeadership

HABITS

Habits are a set of thoughts, behaviours, and ways of being that are developed through repeated behaviour. Habits are formed from the moment we become aware that there is a 'norm' of how to do things. Some we pick up from our parents, guardians, siblings, and influential individuals around us at a very early age. Others we develop for ourselves through the maturing process.

"Look to your parents for your beliefs about the world and yourself – you may be amazed at the similarities."

ClaimYourDestiny.global   #ConsciousLeadership

Once habits are created they can be difficult to break. To break a habit, we must consciously think about doing something different and then do it — which can equal hard work and being uncomfortable.

The thing is, we can all break habits if we really want to. BUT (and there is a big BUT) the unconscious part of our being is there to keep us safe. Any change and it may feel we are under threat and revert quickly to the old ways.

"Talk to your unconscious and ask its permission if you want to change some deep held habits and motivations to do things in a new way."

"Sounds a bit weird? Well it works, try it for yourself."

ClaimYourDestiny.global   #ConsciousLeadership

VALUES

Your values are a central part of who you are and who you want to be. By becoming more aware of these driving motivators in your life, you can use them as a guide to make the best choice in any situation.

Your decisions and actions, when in line with your values, will be easy to make and put into practice. If you are attempting to do something that is not held as a value to you, you will find it harder to do and, potentially, you will be in conflict with yourself.

Here is an example. If one of your values is honesty and you are in a relationship, business or personal, with someone who you know tells untruths, how hard will you find it to trust them? What will this do to your behaviour and your motivation within the relationship?

Values can be worked with, reordered, and installed — so do not lose hope. I personally have needed to work hard on my value regarding money. To say the least, it was slightly askew!

ATTITUDES

Your attitude is a predisposition to respond either negatively or positively towards an idea, object, person, or situation. It is the way you feel about something or someone. It can also be a particular feeling or opinion. It is seen as a conscious behaviour but will come from an unconscious driver.

Your attitude evolves as a result of your beliefs and values and will influence:

- Your choice of action and behaviour

- Your response to challenges

- Your response to incentives

- Your response to a word

- Your response to someone trying to help you

We all have an attitude — we cannot not have one. Generally, when it is said someone has an attitude it is meant as a negative opinion, but attitudes are drivers for good as well. It is just a common adaptation of a word which is more often linked to negativity.

As with anything else we do, our attitude is a choice we make. My choice, and I trust yours as you are reading this book, is to start each day with a positive attitude — it soon becomes a habit.

If you want to change something in your life, surround yourself with those who are on the same path or learn from those who have already done the 'thing' that you want to do. Attitudes are contagious so eradicate those personally held by yourself and those that are owned by people that may be in your circle who aren't helping you. If you don't know what your attitudes are, ask someone for feedback who will tell you the truth.

Also carefully study your close associates to make your own decisions on who stays with you on your journey and who leaves, their attitudes can be contagious. Look at the relationships that are in your life and acknowledge whether they are supporting you or hindering you. Decisions then can be made from a realistic position of what you want to do.

SOCIAL INTELLIGENCE

Social intelligence indicates that portions of our knowledge acquisition can be directly related to observing others within the context of social interactions, experiences and media influences.

So what does this mean to all of us? Basically, it means that if we see something that is rewarded, we copy it so that we get rewarded. We achieve the same result as we have observed, therefore we have achieved our result, which was our goal. There is far more to it but that's the basic concept. We learn by example from others.

So who do we copy? We copy those close to us and we adopt behaviours to fit into the crowd and belong. As we get older, we copy those who we admire or those who we aspire to be like. We develop a sense of self and become more aware of what it is we want. We begin to lead rather than follow — well some of us do and I expect you are a leader since you are reading this book! Join my Facebook group for more, https://www.facebook.com/groups/ClaimYourDestiny/

We are motivated to belong to a group with a certain set of characteristics.

That could be because it is what we want or it can be because we know no different. It can be through peer pressure or choice, but whichever route we take it is ultimately our choice!

Join my Facebook group for more, https://www.facebook.com/groups/ClaimYourDestiny/

It is these drivers of behaviour that make you act differently from, or the same as, others in any given situation. So, by understanding these drivers, you can better understand why you do the things you do. The skill is not only to understand your conscious needs, but also those that are unconscious in nature.

"In the choice between changing one's mind and proving there's no need to do so, most people get busy on the proof."

-John Kenneth Galbraith

SELF-PERCEPTION

Self-perception is the belief or disbelief in our own capabilities to achieve a goal or an outcome. These beliefs provide the foundation for human motivation, well-being, and personal accomplishment. This is because unless you believe that your actions can produce the outcomes you desire, you will have little incentive to act or to persevere in the face of difficulties.

Of course, human functioning is influenced by many factors. The success or failure you experience as you engage the countless tasks that comprise your life naturally influences the many decisions you must make. Also, the knowledge and skills you possess will certainly play critical roles in what you choose to do and not do.

"People's level of motivation, emotional states, and actions are based more on what they believe than on what is objectively true. For this reason, how you behave can often be better predicted by the beliefs you hold about your capabilities than by what you are actually capable of accomplishing."

ClaimYourDestiny.global #ConsciousLeadership

You only need to watch one of the reality TV shows to see how clearly some people are deluded about their own abilities. The opposite is also true — you talk to someone who you know is gifted and they think and believe the complete opposite.

Our upbringing and early influencers, or even a recent happening, have a huge part to play in how and what we believe about ourselves. The great news though is whatever has happened in the past does not have to happen in our future.

These perceptions help determine what you do with the knowledge and skills you have. They also explain why your behaviours are sometimes not matched to your actual capabilities and why your behaviour may differ widely from somebody else, even when you have similar knowledge and skills.

For example, many talented people suffer frequent (and sometimes debilitating) bouts of self-doubt about capabilities they clearly possess, just as many individuals are confident about what they can accomplish despite possessing a modest repertoire of skills. Belief and reality are seldom perfectly matched, and individuals are typically guided by their beliefs when they engage the world.

As a consequence, your accomplishments are generally better predicted by your self-perception than by your previous achievements, knowledge, or skills.

Of course, no amount of confidence or self-appreciation can produce success when requisite skills and knowledge are absent.

"Skills and knowledge can all be gained if you want them enough and you find the right mentor to teach you."

ClaimYourDestiny.global   #ConsciousLeadership

COLLECTIVE PERCEPTION

Because individuals operate collectively as well as individually, self-perception is both a personal and a social construct. Collective systems develop a sense of collective effectiveness, it can create the group's shared belief in its capability to attain goals and accomplish desired tasks.

One brain is one but the collective brainpower of a group equals more than the sum of its parts — it's the adage $1+1=3$ or $2+2 = 5$. However, this is only true when the collective works together in harmony with the same aim. If members of the collective are working against each other one brain doesn't even equate to one — it will function at a lesser capability, as will the individual as they will be experiencing conflict.

For example, organisations develop collective beliefs about the capability of their salesforce to perform, of their managers to teach and otherwise enhance the lives of their workforce, and of their administrators and policymakers to create environments conducive to these tasks. Organisations, as well as individuals, also create beliefs that are not positive — they cannot gain additional sales, clients, revenue, etc. Collectiveness creates a culture which needs to be managed.

Organisations with a strong sense of positive collective perception exercise empowering and vitalising influences over their employees. These effects are evident in their results.

The power of others' attitudes (as mentioned previously) are contagious and will affect your motivation. If you are in the company of a high sender of negative emotion, you will be affected. If you are in the company of a high sender of positivity, it will be less influential.

As the saying goes, it only takes one bad apple to spoil the barrel.

Weed out the bad apples and your motivation will improve. Take on more of the good apples that are doing the same thing that you want to do and your motivation will improve by leaps and bounds.

CHOICES

Only you can justify the choices you make and most of you will make your choices in reference to past experiences rather than future opportunities. Change how you think and you will change your future.

> *"The definition of insanity is doing the same thing over and over again and expecting a different result."*
>
> – Albert Einstein

How do you change to get a different result? It's easy, think differently and take different actions. Open your mind and your being to possibilities; your past does not have to equal your future. With #ConsciousLeadership it can all change.

Every thought, every action, and every decision you make takes you closer to, or further away, from where you want to be. The smallest of decisions compounded over time creates massive change. Rather than attempt to make a huge change overnight, which can be scary and overwhelming, make small incremental changes that lead you towards your goal.

What do I mean? 5 minutes exercise a day wont make much difference if you do or don't do it BUT 5 minutes everyday will. A cake on one day wont make much difference to your health BUT a cake every day will (in the wrong direction). Delaying cutting the lawn for one day wont make much difference BUT delaying every day will.

Even doing nothing takes you further away because everything else is moving forward. The skills of yesteryear will not suffice in the next year. Think about how technology changes. If you haven't kept up with the last change you will soon be a very long way behind!

Sometimes, it can be a life-changing event that allows you to make the decision to do something immediately that you have tried before and failed at. A friend of mine, when diagnosed with cancer, stopped smoking overnight after 40 years. Please do not leave it until that type of thing happens before you change. Take on board #ConsciousLeadership now and change your life for the better, it is your choice!

Start to work now on different decisions for what you want and need:

- Why wait to be taken through a disciplinary process at work before you improve your skills or performance?

- Why wait until you are so over or underweight before you change your nutrition intake?

- Why wait until you cannot walk upstairs without puffing before you increase your fitness level?

- Why wait until you are close to retirement to think about how much money you need to live on and enjoy your retirement?

Through reading, applying, and practicing the experiences of others, you can learn what has worked for those before you, and you can apply those principles in your own life.

Motivational states are directive, they guide behaviours toward satisfying specific goals or specific needs. Do you have clearly defined goals? If you don't, sit down now, identify what it is you really want or need, and write that down. Then create a plan of how you will achieve it. This will provide you with motivation to do things differently.

If you want more information on how to this, I can highly recommend my book 'The Life Changing Magic of Setting Goals'. It is available from Amazon or through ClaimYourDestiny.global

"Change begins with your awareness that your beliefs are a choice; all beliefs, conscious or unconscious, are based on a choice."

ClaimYourDestiny.global   #ConsciousLeadership

There are a myriad of choices to be made all of the time. If you choose a different way to do something, gather information that allows you to make an educated choice for action. Do your research and due diligence and pick the best solution for you.

This will enhance your confidence, create new knowledge, quieten the inner doubting voice, match your values, enhance your beliefs, or question them to bolster your attitude.

This will allow you to convince your unconscious that you are looking after it and it will help you. Provide your unconscious with the reason why you are making alternate choices to that of the past and it will support you all the way.

DELAYED GRATIFICATION

There have been many studies done related to the benefits of delayed gratification. What does this really mean? It means living with the future in mind rather than the present.

In this world of instant gratification, keeping up with the Joneses, wearing the right designer labels, being influenced by adverts that say you must have this face cream and that aftershave, feeling like your holidays must become bigger and more expensive, having to change your car every two years, etc. It can be hard to resist the instant temptation, to be outside the norm, or to exclude yourself from your friends' activities.

In the moment, sometimes it can seem obvious to take the reward, and worry about the future in the future.

Your choice is dependent on your goals, your drivers, your beliefs (and how strong they are), and how strong your will to resist temptation is.

If you can recognise when you have an opportunity for a larger or more important reward, it shows you know the difference between your needs and your wants. When you can recognise these situations, there are key terms you must think of.

Patience, will, and self-control are all characteristics of people who are masters of their environment. One common challenge is postponing immediate gratification in the pursuit of long-term goals. Delayed gratification is the process of transcending immediate temptations to achieve long-term goals.

Knowing how to create, manage, and control your goals is the first step towards completing the things you want most in life; with a goal, we engage our brain to work toward it.

Think of goals as roadmaps designed to keep you on target. They make the experience and the journey possible and more enjoyable. They, in fact, become priorities that drive our actions. They become motivators.

Let me ask you once again:

- What are your long-term goals? And for some of you

- What are your short-term goals?

If you do not have goals sit down now and plan them for yourself, tell yourself and others they are important, write them down and believe you are worthy of them and you will achieve them. Focus on them and they will become a reality

THE POWER OF QUESTIONS

Questions, when constructed in the right way, are the most powerful way to access your beliefs. And this works irrespective of who asks the question. Ask yourself a question and your mind will do its best to provide you with an answer. The better your question, the better the answer.

Do you want to spend the rest of your life figuring out how to get the things you desire, or would you rather put all the guesswork behind you and get down to the fun of building an out-of-this-world lifestyle? Easy choice, right? Then do yourself a favour: suspend your disbelief, lower your shields, and try a simple way of improving your life.

Identify someone you respect who's already experiencing what you're after, find out what questions they habitually ask themselves to achieve those experiences, then use those questions yourself.

This is a globally powerful approach to success that can get you the things you want more quickly than anything else I've discovered. The habitual questions that others ask themselves when asked by yourself, to yourself can transform your life. You don't even need to understand how it all works really, although the answer's quite simple:

"When you change your habitual questions, you change your beliefs, when you change your beliefs, you change your actions, when you change your actions you change your results."

ClaimYourDestiny.global   #ConsciousLeadership

Try it! Take the time to prove to yourself that it works, that it can change the level of pain and pleasure in your life. If you like the results, keep using the questions you've discovered until they become second nature. Do this and you won't care about the why's and the wherefore's. You'll be too busy! You'll have learned firsthand there's nothing more powerful than a good question followed by action.

Ask different questions, and you will end up thinking different thoughts, saying different words, taking different actions, and getting different results. When you go one step further by modeling the questions of successful people, you're helping to ensure that the different results you're pursuing are also good results. In other words, you've done everything you can to arrive at a different place — a good place — to develop different beliefs, which are also profitable beliefs, and to become a different person who is more like the people you admire.

FOCUS

So what does all this mean really?

It means that by looking at why you do what you do and the beliefs behind that, you can basically change the thoughts and motives that direct your behaviour so that you achieve a different result, start a new job, get a promotion, create your own business, leave a relationship, start a relationship, have that difficult conversation, learn to swim, fly a plane, or simply eat a new food; the list is endless.

It is your choice completely — where your focus goes your energy flows — so change your focus to change your results.

Some of our important choices have a timeline. If you delay a decision, the opportunity is gone forever. Sometimes your doubts will stop you from making a choice that involves change and an opportunity may be missed. If you really truly want to change, start now — now is as good a time as any.

Create and ClaimYourDestiny.global through #ConsciousLeadership

My Facebook page and group is ClaimYourDestiny or you can follow me on Twitter @JulieHogbin. Visit ClaimYourDestiny.global for more articles and up to date information, plus various other social media channels and Linkedin. My hashtag is #ConsciousLeadership if you would like to find me.

Motives and motivation are a matter of choice — yours! Choose well, look at why you believe what you believe, and question it. Listen to the answers of the questions you ask and you will create a different future if you really want to.

My final questions to you are:

- How much do you want to change?

- How willing are you to do what is required?

- What do you need to do right now?

Good luck with whatever it is you want to do. Here's to your fabulous success; you know where to find me.

Julie xx

Twice the Retirement for Half the Effort

A Baby Boomer's Guide to Profitable Apartment Investing

DR. JAMES MCQUISTON

L et's face it. There are many so-called experts in property investing, and there is no dearth of information on how to make it rich...quick. When push comes to shove, very few retirees make it beyond the first property investment, let alone to the top of the property ladder.

Why you may ask? You're smart and savvy, you've made it so far and are sitting on top of a very nice nest-egg. You most certainly won't make the same mistakes that have dogged those less lucky. However, from our viewpoint as property investors, the field or property investing is riddled with potholes for beginners.

Here are some of the common pitfalls: making a decision based on emotions rather than hard, cold facts, rushing in without doing sufficient homework just because someone else appeared interested in the same property. On the other hand, you could be procrastinating so much that the property is snapped up by other more astute investors. And the most common blight of all on beginning investors?

Poor cash flow management. Not understanding the costs involved in buying and holding onto property. Not accounting for or failing to plan and set aside funds for unexpected contingencies. Such contingencies include unplanned maintenance repairs, extended vacancies, bad tenants, high turnover rates. Then again, there is choosing the wrong type of property, in the wrong neighborhood, at the wrong time of the investing cycle by buying high and selling low.

I'm not saying that property investing is not for baby boomers. On the contrary, investing in property, significantly in apartments, is a proven strategy to accumulate wealth and generate handsome double-digit returns. You have to do it right.

WILL YOUR MONEY LAST AS LONG AS YOU?

Now as a baby boomer, you've some very real concerns. If your money is relatively dormant, you may not be earning more than 4% and the most important question you have is:

How long will your money last?

The math is not in your favour. According to the Employment Benefits Research Institute (ebri.org), 43% of baby boomers are at risk of running out of money. Our figures show that by the age of 75, at least half the baby boomers will run out of money. How much you take out of your retirement savings each year will affect how long the money will last.

Of course, if you draw down by 4% every year, your retirement savings will last for 25 years. But will a 4% withdrawal rate be sufficient for the lifestyle you've grown accustomed to? The numbers tell all. If you've saved $250,000, withdrawing 4% a year means you have to live off $10,000 for 12 months. If you take out much more, your money will run out faster! The numbers tell all. (see Table 1)

Increasing your withdrawal rate to 6% means you will run dry in 16.6 years and to 8% implies that you will have no savings left in 12.5 years. Not an optimistic picture, is it?

In Table 1, which displays the relationship between annual withdrawal rates from savings and time left to the portfolio, we assume $250,000 in retirement savings and an annual appreciation in the portfolio equal to inflation.

Table 1: **Impact of Differing Withdrawal Rates on a $250,000 Retirement Portfolio**

Withdrawal Rate	Annual Withdrawals	Time in years before money runs out
4%	$10,000	25
6%	$15,000	16.6
8%	$20,000	12.5
10%	$25,000	10

LEVERAGING TO GET DOUBLE DIGIT RETURNS

In a Federal Reserve Survey of Consumer Finances completed in 2012, it showed that equities account for a substantial part of assets held by baby boomers. In fact, the Investment Company Institute in a recent Wall Street Journal reports that more than a quarter of investors have 100% of their IRA's invested in stocks – including those between 60 and 64 years old. Another 16% have 80% of their IRA's invested in the stock market. However, how much of a return have these investors derived from stocks?

Figures of indexed funds offered to the public sector through The Federal Thrift Savings Plans showed domestic stocks posted an average of 7.44% returns over the past 10 years. Small stocks did better with a 10.4% return but bonds and money markets only returned between 3.4%-4.6% to investors every year for 10 years.

The issue is if inflation is 3% a year, how safe are your 4% returns? Not very secure is the answer. With such concerns to address, how do you go about changing the math in your favor?

The answer lies in leveraged appreciation, which you create by implementing these four steps.
1.   Buy undervalued properties with upside potential
2.   Upgrade the properties and raise rents accordingly
3.   Leverage the property through financing
4.   Pay off the mortgage through rental payments from tenants

Apartment complexes are valued differently from residential properties. When you are shopping around for a house, the appraiser will value it according to the most recent transactions of houses of comparable sizes in your neighborhood. An apartment complex, on the other hand, is determined by the cash flow i.e. the rental income received less any outgoings for maintenance, debt service, management, and property taxes.

Therefore, if you can find an apartment complex, which is overdue for a remodel or facelift, in a nice neighborhood and which is struggling with a 70% occupancy rate, you are well-poised to earn double digit returns.

Let's walk through how it works in real life.

You find an apartment with deferred maintenance and high vacancy near 70%; since it is a little shabby and out of style, you are likely to buy it for at least a 20% discount. You put a down payment of 33 1/3 % of the negotiated price.

Next, you remodel the unoccupied units and when leases expire and the tenants move out, you upgrade those units and raise rents by 4% across the board. This process spreads out over four years to give time for existing leases to terminate, for phased remodeling and for the increased rents to take root, so to speak.

Here is how you gain leverage through borrowings. If you put a down payment of 33 1/3% and borrow the remaining 66 2/3%, you have established a 3:1 leverage. In other words, if the apartment complex was worth $1,000,000, you put down $333,000 but because you control the ownership of 100% of the building, you get all the benefits, such as higher rents that accrue to the entire upgraded building. (As an aside, making at least a 30% down payment opens up access to better financing terms and you won't have to pay such high interest rates on your borrowings)

Therefore, when you raise rents by 4% a year, you realize a gain of 4% on your down payment AND a gain 8% on your leveraged position, that is that portion of the investment financed with other people's money, greatly magnifying the returns on your apartment building.

Proceeding with this example, let's also say you amortize your debt over 25 years with 2% of the mortgage retired yearly

In summary, your annual rate of appreciation on your investment is made up of 4 components; remember we are assuming a 4-year holding period:

1. Purchase at 20% discount, amortized over 4 years. 5%

2. Increased rents after remodeling 4%

3. 8% on leveraged position (see above paragraphs) 8%

4. 2% of the borrowings paid off annually. 2%

Total annual appreciation 19%

The conclusion: In this example, using leverage significantly boosts your rate of return in apartment investing. By smart and strategic use of leverage in an appreciating asset, like apartment complexes, you are substantially increasing your net worth. Here is one more thought. In all likelihood, with the renovations enhancing the desirability of your building, you will attract more tenants and increase the occupancy rate from 70% to 90%. The higher occupancy rate translates to higher cash flow which, in turn boosts the value of the apartment complex by at least 20%.

The previous example is for demonstration purposes only and is no guarantee of future performance.

STRIKING IT HOT

Many investors have become wealthy through investing in apartments. However, those new to property investing in this sector hold the misperception that you require millions to make millions in apartment investing.

What if I told you that you can gain entry into this lucrative field and enjoy double-digit returns with as little as $25,000? Here is a chance to copy the moves of millionaires without having to start out with millions of your own money. Isn't that exciting and definitely worth exploring?

We titled this chapter *Twice The Retirement for Half The Effort* because we have proven it time and time again that investing in apartment complexes does work. Everyone needs a home and people don't move out just because the economy turns sour. If anything, a slower economy encourages downsizing from large houses with excess capacity to more affordable apartment living. With tenants on a lease, you receive a steady stream of cash flow; if you own a residential property as an investment, when the lease ends, you have no cash flow until you find a new tenant. Looking at your investment options in this light, apartment investing would appear to spread the risk over more rental units than putting your money into residential properties.

How would you then maximize your retirement savings to benefit from such kinds of leveraged appreciation?

First off, opt for a self-directed IRA. It gives you the option to safely control your own investments and to tax-defer any gains.

Next, you want to have your real estate team in place before you begin a search for property. You want to line up the financiers, the underwriters, the brokers, lawyers, property managers and contractors (for any renovations) because the real estate investor with the best professional resources will know which properties to ignore and which deserve careful consideration.

However, rather than assemble a group of professionals on your own steam, one plodding step at a time, we at United Equity Partners (UEP) offer you a ready-made team that has proven skills and a track record in successful investing. With our deep-domain expertise in real estate, we focus on underperforming niche markets with assets available for sale below market price.

You may have heard of Real Estate Investment Trusts (REITs) that promise a steady dividend payout. These large trusts focus on Grade A apartment buildings or other assets like office towers and shopping malls, which are already income producing and which require minimal maintenance and renovation. However, REITs pay a premium to invest in such quality buildings, which suggest that there is limited scope for asset appreciation.

HOW WE GET IT RIGHT AT TWICE THE RETIREMENT FOR HALF THE EFFORT

There is a common classification of property in commercial investing in which properties are categorized as A, B or C. At UEP, we have made a deliberate and strategic investment decision to focus on medium Class C and C+ apartments in B neighborhoods. Class C are properties which are older and which could significantly benefit from upgrades and renovations and even a change in management; B neighborhoods reflect a higher quality of consumers who will apply to live in the upgraded apartments.

Our strategy is to buy below market price and through careful upgrading and renovation, we add more value to the apartment complex than we have spent. The owners of these C or C+ properties are often either banks left holding foreclosures or distressed owners who are unable to service their debt or are tired of holding on to their underperforming assets. UEP takes them off their hands at a price that is fair to both parties.

We run through the figures carefully before inviting our future equity partners to join us. We handle our partner's money more conservatively than if it were our own before purchasing properties that UEP affiliates will manage. In our team of professionals are onsite managers who know how to add value through selected renovations, who know how much of a rent increase we can get after upgrades are completed and how to create incentives to attract a desirable class of tenants. Our underwriters perform the appropriate calculations to weigh risks against returns and will not make an offer on the property until we have conducted appropriate research and due diligence.

IS PROPERTY INVESTING RIGHT FOR ME?

If you are willing to hold an investment for the medium term to realize appreciable gains, you are right for apartment investing. Our holding period is 3-5 years. Of course, you may get faster returns in the stock market, but you have to make sure you buy early and sell at the right time before the markets top out. If you pull the trigger at the wrong time, it takes a considerable length of time to make good what you've lost. For example, to recover from a 20% loss, you need a 25% gain to break even. If you have suffered a drawdown on your capital of 25%, you need a 33% gain just to get back to your original capital. In order words, you need three right decisions to make up the losses from one wrong move.

Many retail investors in the stockmarket have been feeling that they have been served a raw deal. Not surprisingly. With technology like high frequency trading where sophisticated computerized programs make thousands of buy and sell decisions in less time than it took you to read half this sentence, and with billion dollar hedge funds influencing price and volumes, you are right to feel that way.

Bonds are predictable but after accounting for inflation, your bonds could be worth less at the end of the contract than when you first invested. In property investing, you need to be invested for a longer time, but if you choose correctly, your income stream is significantly less volatile and definitely more predictable since leases are typically signed for at least a year, if not more.

Further, at UEP, we tailor and align our investments to your objectives. We interview our investors to find out more about your investment expectations before inviting you to become equity partners in the appropriate portfolio of apartment investments.

All the professionals in our team are fully invested in making sure you are successful. Unlike in stockmarket funds where you have to pay a sales load to gain entry, we don't make money until you do. That differentiates us from other property investing funds. We work hard at seeking out investments that will produce a high enough profit margin so that everyone involved is profitably compensated.

WHY SHOULD I WORK WITH A TEAM?

We have an extensive network among banks, brokers, financiers, lawyers and contractors that an individual investor will find difficult to approximate. Remember the investor with the right combination of resources is able to move quickly when the right opportunities spring up. Being able to close a transaction fast enough is a significant advantage in any market, especially in properties.

We have established relationships with banks that have an inventory of homes and apartments, so we have access to good deals well before the individual investor gets wind of these opportunities. Brokers are willing to give us first look at new properties because they know that UEP has both the financial capacity and the willingness to close on desirable transactions. Finally, we are able to call on contractors who give us priority in remodeling because we provide them with consistent work.

If you were to undertake renovations on your own, how would you be able to gauge that the contractor is bidding accurately and is not going to surprise you, unpleasantly, with cost overruns when the final bill is to be paid?

That's what we mean that with UEP, you get *Twice the Retirement for Half the Effort*. We put in all the hard work so you don't have to.

Here is an analogy I would like to share. When your car runs into problems, your first thought is to get it to the mechanic, isn't it? You don't instead think about buying a repair manual, get tools and diagnostic equipment, find a garage with a lift and get your hands all greasy and dirty. Unless you have the training and mindset of a car mechanic, you are likely not to be able to diagnose, troubleshoot and repair your car, not even if you are armed to the hilt with D-I-Y tutorials. Of course, you won't waste your time attempting to be your own car repairman because the mechanic is worth every dollar that you pay. You know without a doubt that he will be able to diagnose the problem and get it fixed, freeing you to focus on the important things that matter.

With that being said, why not go to the experts when it comes to investing in apartments? You reap the benefits of collective experience and significant economies of scale and every dollar you invest comes back to you multiplied.

Find out more about how to build your retirement wealth faster than you would be able to achieve on your own by visiting us at http://unitedequitypartners.com/. We have a wealth of free bonuses and tips on ways for you to make money in apartment investing. Take advantage of these ideas to accumulate wealth that you may be able to retire comfortably and confidently, secure in the knowledge that money will be there when you need it. It is time to take action to build your wealth responsibly, so act now, visit our website or email me at Mcquiston1999@gmail.com.

Dr. James McQuiston is a Senior Managing Partner of United Equity Partners, who identifies and selects real estate and business opportunities for the firm. Although he started out as an optometrist, he showed great skill and enjoyed significant success in commercial real estate investing and from that foundation, expanded his investments into residential and commercial properties in Texas, Oklahoma and Illinois. He has also co-founded an association of stock investors and managed several portfolios of blue-chip stocks. He donates his optometric skills to the underprivileged around the world and has been actively involved with Eye Projects on four continents.

How to Make Your Advertisement Infinitely More Effective

FRANCIS ABLOLA

What we're going to talk about in this chapter is how to focus a laser beam on your target audience when advertising. It's not going to be about writing your sales letter and writing your copy. I'm a direct response copywriter. What that means is I write copy that produces results immediately. But before any single word is written on a page, I want to make sure that I have the audience in mind. How do I do this? Through mind reading. I know it's a little funny to talk about mind reading, but How to Make Your Advertisement Infinitely More Effective is really about getting inside the customer's mind and figuring out exactly what that individual desires. There's a quote I want to share with you. It's by Robert Collier, who's one of the greatest copywriters to ever live. It states, "Always enter the conversation already taking place in the customer's mind."

Now if you're not taking notes right now, you should be. I want you to write this down … "Always enter the conversation already taking place in the customer's mind." Because as we go through each day, all of us have something that's so pressing in our heads that we need to just get it out into the world. If someone can actually go in there, into our heads, and solve the problem for us, the one that we're thinking about constantly, it immediately cuts through the clutter of everyday thinking and allows them to really reach us. So, that's what we're going to talk about, how you can get into the customer's mind with your marketing.

My promise for everybody reading this is that I'm going to walk you through some powerful influence strategies for increasing the effectiveness of any marketing, of any business or any stage of business. If you're just getting started, you need to know this information; if you've been in business for years, if you're a veteran, and you're not doing this in your business right now, you're leaving money on the table because your advertising is not as effective as it could be.

Did you ever wish that you were a super hero? I think we all might have at some time in our lives. And as a marketer there's one super power that I would want and that's the ability to read people's minds. I would want to get into their heads and actually figure out what they want, even if they, themselves, don't truly know what they want. That's really what we're going to talk about today. It's marketing mind reading.

Now imagine having the power to focus only on attracting your ideal customers, having the ability to build trust instantly with everyone you work with, being able to stay on top of the mind of someone who's looking at your advertising, someone who could be a potential customer of yours, with the power to channel existing wants and desires into your business.

Let's say your business already channels the existing wants and desires of your customers. Can you imagine having the power to press all their emotional hot buttons and psychological triggers so that you send them into a buying frenzy? Wouldn't you like that?

Businesspeople—they have a product, it's their baby. They like to think they know everything that everybody wants, but it's simply not the truth. Yet, that's what we're going to go into today. Imagine having a magical marketing crystal ball that tells you exactly how your ideal customer is thinking and feeling. Now we all can't have that magic ball, but you can use top secret intelligence to create irresistible advertising that fuels your business.

I'm super excited to share that top secret intelligence with you today. When you do these things, you make your ideal customers pay attention. Now, we're so bombarded with information, it's hard to focus on anything. But if you really make your ideal customers pay attention to you, that's a very, very strong thing you can do. They should see you as a trusted advisor and a friend and an authority. Being an authority in your marketplace is a must. Being able to turn that authority into more leads, more loyal customers and eventually more sales, well that's the ultimate super power.

I think everybody reading this wants more sales, so I hope you're with me on that. It really doesn't matter if you're just getting started, if you've been in business for decades or what nature of industry you're in. A lot of people say, "Well, my business is different." Using this strategy, this thing I'm about to show you, every business is the same—because human nature is the same. And that's really what we're planning on using in our advertising.

What I want to show you today is going to help you make an immediate, dramatic impact to your product. But before we go on, I want to answer the question: who the heck is this guy? Some of my early mentors were Les Brown, the legendary Jim Rohn (who was the mentor of Tony Robbins) and William Bailey (who was the mentor Les Brown and Jim Rohn). Today, I'm considered a top marketing and advertising strategist. I work with Fortune 1000 companies, and I've also worked with garage start-ups. Lots of multimillion-dollar CEOs, and New York Times best-selling authors. I've been featured in papers and websites all around the country. I'm also the number-one Amazon best selling author of The Art and Science of Success, with many other best-selling authors. The gurus actually call on me to produce more revenue for their advertising campaigns. This strategy that I'm sharing with you, is going to help you do the same. I've helped my clients create millions in revenue, hundreds of thousands of new leads and customers in rapid speed.

But none of that stuff really matters. What really matters is getting what's inside of my head working for you as if you had a mini me helping grow your business. Let's really get started, because everything we're going to show is actionable, and immediately beneficial to you.

Here's the big problem: we're all overloaded with information. We're overloaded, you're overloaded, your prospects and your customers are overloaded. It's been said that we are bombarded with some 3000 advertisements per day. How do we get our prospect's attention? That's really what we're fighting for with everything going on in the world today. The first solution that everyone goes to is advertise. But how do we know we're doing the right thing? There are so many things we can do ... TV, radio, internet, social media, press releases and online classified ads. There are so many different channels as a marketer, and as an advertiser, that we can use. But how do we know it's effective? How do we know we're using our time the right way? How do we know we're using our money the right way? As an entrepreneur, I'm sure you'd agree that money and time are the two most important things in a business.

So really what we want to do is focus in on effective advertising. And here's what effective advertising does … Effective advertising focuses on the right media to the right potential customer. If your advertising doesn't do that, if it goes to a broad audience, you may be losing money. Does your advertisement speak directly to your target audience? Effective advertising speaks to the person who's reading it. Not only that, but it is benefit driven to what your ideal customer wants. Not what the marketer wants but what they're customer is looking for. And finally, it has a specific call-to-action. If you're advertising doesn't do this, you may be leaving money on the table.

As an example, you wouldn't stick a realtor sign up on the front lawn of a home to attract a million-dollar buyer, would you? Really, it's comparing your advertising to a shotgun, versus a sniper rifle. All of your advertising should be the sniper rifle, especially if you have a small budget to work with.

Here's the bad news: all of your customers are ignoring you. You really need to cut through the clutter. You need to get their attention with laser focus and that sniper rifle approach. So, who do your customers listen to? I've eluded to this earlier, they listen to trusted friends and advisors. They listen to people who understand their needs, their problems and have their best interest in mind. David Ogilvy, one of my legendary heroes in marketing, wrote, "All good marketing requires empathy." It's very important, it's another writer-downer, if you're taking notes. "All good marketing requires empathy." That means having a connection with your target audience but calling them a person, because that's what they really are.

So how do you reach all these real people? Too many business owners tend to get their advertising and their marketing done the wrong way. One of the ways they get marketing done wrong is they try to sell the features and not the benefits of what someone is looking for. They market to what they think is important verses what the customer's looking for. They don't think what the customer thinks is important.

Now, there may be some people out there thinking, "Well, that's not me. I didn't do this when I started my marketing campaigns, and we're making a lot of good money right now." But the fact is, it doesn't matter if you're losing money or making money, if you don't know your customer market—even if you're doing well with your marketing—chances are you can probably increase your sales and conversions. It doesn't always mean you're going to fail by not using this approach first, but it almost always means you're going to increase conversions by going back and doing this kind of research.

Here's what I want to stress today. You can be a terrible advertisement copywriter, but as long as you know your market with pinpoint accuracy, you can create effective advertising. My advice might seem counter-intuitive ... and that's to stop selling to customers. Instead, you want to listen to your customers, and you want to become their best friends, their BFFs. The reason why is because you want to position yourself as a trusted advisor offering valuable guidance to your best friend. That puts you in a completely different category from all the people who aren't listening to your market but are just trying to sell to them.

When you become a trusted advisor, you become the first person this customer listens to. You become their expert and their authority. You become your target market--thinking what they think, feeling what they feel, going where they go, and experiencing what they experience.

Now, I became a really good copywriter in my niche, but not because I'm a great writer. In fact, I barely made it out of college English. I barely made it out of high school. The reason I became a really good copywriter in my niche is because I understand what my audience is looking for. I actually go to seminars as an attendee to talk with the people who are there, to do my market research, to get into their heads, to feel what they feel and to experience what they experience.

If you're selling to a market, and it's your primary market, you want to become that market, not a person selling to them. This is so vitally important. Stop thinking customer, prospect, or name on a list. Start thinking "real person" with hopes, dreams, wants, needs, desires, and problems only you can solve.

I have a funny approach to doing this that I call making up "imaginary best friends" for fun and profit. Because I love my best friends. And becoming someone's best friend is the next best thing to climbing into their head and reading their mind. Again, going back to the super powers that we all wish we had, mine is being able to read somebody's mind. If you can't read somebody's mind, the next best thing is becoming best friends with them, because best friends tell each other secrets. They tell each other hopes and dreams and desires. They let you know what they want, why they want it, what they like, who they trust, why they trust them, and why they buy.

If I consider you a really good friend, we share things that we wouldn't share to the general public. And I'm sure people reading this today have the same thing with their best friend. So, I want you to imagine being best friends with your marketplace. And here's the thing, your imaginary best friends? What we do is call it creating customer personas, or often times creating customer avatars. Basically, it's a clear, written profile of specific segments of your target audience.

151

When you have this, you can actually identify to the "T" who the person your ideal customer is. You want to focus on attracting who will give you the most money with the least resistance. This may seem like I'm saying you should get more for doing less. But it's not; it's about making the most money with the least amount of resistance.

Zero in on your best customers. Zero in on the people who you enjoy working with, and who also enjoy working with you. Think about it … Would you rather work with the guy who enjoys going golfing a couple of afternoons per week, or another guy, the party animal? The answer really depends on what you want and what you have to offer. But the marketing is different, the advertising is different, to go after these two different groups of people. When you're creating imaginary friends, it really helps to interact with your target customer on a deeper, individual basis. After all, what you're doing here is building a lifestyle business.

You always want to think in terms of what benefits they want, not what you can offer them; not what you think they want, but what they're actually looking for. You must remember this for when you get into the marketplace, for when you create these imaginary friends, for when you truly begin to understand what they're looking for, because you might come to find out they're looking for something completely different than what you have to offer and that they're only working with you because that's the closest thing. This is exciting, because you now have the opportunity to get more money or work from them by creating a different relationship—all because they're looking for something that's not on the market. Who knows? This could even be a new opportunity for you and your business.

Creating imaginary friends also guides your marketing: it guides your brand, it guides design, and it guides advertising messages that speak to the proper audience. Again, we're seeing the shotgun versus the sniper rifle approach. So let's make some imaginary friends. I'm about to walk you through a process that I use whenever I create a marketing piece for a new audience, or a new market.

I'd like to say I'm not alone, because I have my imaginary friends who are helping me write my marketing. Again, this is the guide to effective advertising, even before writing a single word on a page, or creating a single ad. It's creating these imaginary friends, who tell you exactly what your market's looking for.

STEP 1

The first step is to brainstorm. It's sitting down with a pad and paper and just thinking. "Who are your best customers? Who are they currently? What type of customers do you want to attract? Who would you consider a best customer for you?" When you create these imaginary friends, think of them as they fit into each segment of your customer base. You don't need only one imaginary best friend, you can have multiple imaginary friends who all speak to a different audience.

You want to give them names and personalities, even jobs and families. Be very specific with the information you already know. If you already have customers, you can say, "Well, this is Bob. Bob works full-time, but he also works on the side as a real estate investor. He's looking to be more effective. You know, Bob works 40 hours a week in his regular job, and he spends about 20 hours a week in his real estate investing business. He also has a family and two kids that he tries to juggle with, and he's very frustrated with the results he's getting in this side business."

Knowing all this information, you get to know Bob a little bit better, and how to help him even more. So far this is really just an educated guess, because the next thing you want to do is actually go out in market and prove it. You want to go gather the data. You want to see, do these people really exist? The best way to do that is to actually go and look to your existing customers, go and talk to them. Talk to anybody in your company who interacts with your customers on a daily basis. If you have sales people in your company, for example, talk to them. Maybe talk to them about their best customers.

If you have a best customer in mind, talk to them, ask them what they want. Start doing interviews. The best thing you can do, the easiest thing, is you can survey your list by using a tool like SurveyMonkey or Wufoo. These let you create free forms to send out via email, asking your list of "friends" questions that will help you get to know them better. And by getting to know them better, your advertising becomes much more effective, because you gear all of your marketing message directly to these friends. This is actually how I won the award for copywriter of the year and became the guru's go-to guy. In my market I write heavily to people who want to learn how to become real estate investors. So I go where they go, and I get to know them. I actually go to seminars and sit in the back of the room. I talk to people who are attending—just like I was the seminar for the first time.

I get to know them better, and I find ways to understand them better, to feel what they feel, to understand their emotions, to experience the experiences they go through. And by doing that you discover so many things about your target market that you'll never know just from graphs and data and not seeing customers face-to-face. It's super important to do this, to get to know them and become friends with them. Open up a conversation (and it's amazing to know what kinds of information people give just by opening up a conversation).

STEP 2

The next step is to dig deeper. From the information you've gathered, from the brainstorming you've done and from all the proof you've backed it up with, you want to ... understand who they are, what they want, how they buy, why they buy, and what would get them to buy from you? Obviously, this is a very important question.

STEP 3

Now is the time to create your customer profile. That's right: create a profile of your imaginary friends, and make them as real as possible. I even go to the extent of finding a picture that best represents the person. I actually go to Google images or use a service like iStockphoto or Dreamstime. If you know your target market is male, in his 40s or 50s, with a family, you can actually go to istockphoto.com and find photos of people just like that.

By having these profiles and by getting them as real as possible, you can create this avatar, this persona, this imaginary friend who you can speak to and write to. Just the other day, we were talking to one of my copywriter friends on an interview we did, and he was referencing another copywriter who's a very successful copywriter. On her first promotion she was writing to a market her mother actually fit into. So as her customer avatar, as her persona, and as her imaginary friend, she actually set a picture of her mom in front of her laptop, and as she wrote the letter and the advertising piece, she wrote it as if she was writing to her mother. The advertisement piece was a well-liked hit, and it was very, very successful. Imagine you're writing your advertising to someone you truly care about, who you truly want to see a difference in. This is when and why your advertising becomes so much more powerful.

Here's what you want to ask when you're really digging into creating these imaginary friends. The first one is demographics, it's the who they are. Let's say this is Bob. What do we want to know about Bob? We want to know where he lives, his age group, marital status, occupation, job status and income. Does he own a home, does he rent? What's his education and reading level? That's really important, especially when you're creating an advertisement. What kind of lifestyle does he live? What kind of things interest him? What are his special interests? Maybe it's political interest, something like that. And political affiliations are very important to know, because obviously political affiliations really drive a person's character and how they operate. For example, you don't want to write a message that has a Democrat overtone to a Republican audience. It doesn't work that way.

STEP 4

The next thing is psychographics. This is about what they want and how they see themselves. What's their personal attitude toward themselves? Are they confident or are they not confident about their future? How do you use that in your advertising? How do they interact with you and other people? What are their personality types? Are they outgoing or are they soft-spoken? It's really important to know how to approach a target audience through their certain mannerisms. What are their beliefs? Again, really important. You want to make sure that you're not offending your target audience, but you also don't want to go too soft and make them ignore your advertising. What kind of affiliations in other groups do they have? What's their social status? Where do they see themselves in the world, and how the world reacts to them? What kind of books do they enjoy reading? This is really important. You're getting back into the conversation that's going in their head. If you know they're a huge Twilight fan (Twilight was a huge book on the market), you could actually use Twilight in your advertisement—maybe as a subject line? What websites have they visited? Also note that they're diehard Huffington Post readers. Why? If you've created an advertisement that actually talked about the Huffington Post it would attract them and actually get them to open the advertisement. What kind of hobbies do they do? Again, if they have strong beliefs in a certain hobby, how do you use that in your marketing? And what drives them on a day-to-day basis? Note: All these questions are important, but I think more important than the demographic information, is what they want and how they interact with you.

I also want to add a quick word about websites. I love forums. I love forums because people go to forums to talk with somebody in the same exact niche. It's two people having a conversation who are friends. Everybody chimes in, so you get to know your market well. Dashboards.com is a great website for finding niche forums like that. People open up and act like themselves inside of forums because they're not buying stuff. They feel like they can talk like they would normally talk to their friends. A point to add to the forums is that when people interact on forums, they're actually hidden by their usernames. They can even share their deepest feelings. This goes back to getting into where your market goes. It's not even real life, person-to-person, but it's going to allow you to see them where they spend time and interact with others. Very important, I love this strategy.

Going back to the point of what drives them on a day-to-day basis, what do they focus on? Are they focusing on just surviving a daily life? Or are they looking to connect with others? Are they looking for affluence and significance in their family life? Are they looking for enjoyment on a daily basis? When you understand the true psychological need, what they need to fulfill, your advertising becomes much more effective.

STEP 5

Find the pain. What's really eating away at them, day and night? What's the primary need your imaginary friend is desperate to fill? What's the biggest problem that's always on their mind? What keeps them up at night? Get into the conversation that's already happening on an everyday basis. What problems are they trying to solve in their lives? What's the biggest benefit they want? When you start thinking of what needs they are desperate to fill, and approaching your marketing that way, it becomes so much more effective because it clears the clutter. It stops you from saying "Here's what I think is important to you," but, rather, allows you to say, "This is what seems to be important from your point of view." You begin to be able to understand what influences their decisions. Again, this is a very important part of understanding who your customer is and what is their ultimate goal in buying from or interacting with you. Why are they looking to buy this product or service, if they don't know that they want to buy this product or service? What needs are they looking to fill that will get them to respond to your advertising? What emotions do you want them to feel? Is it security, is it confidence? Do you want them to feel significant when they work with you or buy your product or service? Do you want to give them independence? Are they looking for independence when they buy or interact with you? Also is it fun for them? What would make it fun to work with you? Again, a very important thing to know. Do they trust you? Hopefully the message that has woven its way throughout this entire presentation will lead you to understand that the whole point is getting your customers to trust you as an advisor they can call upon and lean on. And finally, if they don't trust you yet, what has to happen for them to trust you? What are they looking for as a symbol of trust?

A good example of that last point is your mailbox. How many things do you get in the mail for free? People who are sending you free gifts are putting you in a "wow" state of mind, like, "This guy's great. He just gave me something free." It automatically breaks down barriers. But it's also building value upfront, so you have their trust later. This is very, very important. How do you stand out? How do you create that "wow" experience? How are you different? And how do you create that trust to carry you into a deeper relationship. When you're creating that trust, you want to create your trust with your ideal client, which takes us into what we we're going to talk about now, which is how do you focus only on your imaginary friend, who you can help and, more importantly, who wants your help? You can't help everyone, especially if they don't want to hear from you.

So how do you only work with those people who are actively looking for what you have to offer? How do you invest your time and energy on clients and customers who can help expand your business and move in the direction that you want? The answer? You only focus on working with clients and consumers who want that same thing you are offering and who will also support your lifestyle in terms of that.

You also want to avoid time wasters. Don't work with energy vampires, because these people will take your business away from you. Only focus on the imaginary friends, the customer group that most wants your help, and that you can help the most by giving them massive transformational value.

STEP 6

Put your imaginary friends to work. Now that you've created all these profiles, that you've put these pieces together, how do you put them to work?

The simplest thing is, think of your new imaginary friend every time you plan a new campaign, or craft, or sales message. Again, all of your advertising is driven (laser-focused) to that specific person. So as you're creating your marketing, as you're creating your websites and as you're creating your copy, think of, "Does my imaginary friend, or will my imaginary friend, respond to this piece of advertising?"

The next thing is to speak to that individual. Here's a trick: all of your advertisements should speak to an individual person, not a group. Because when we read advertisements, we don't feel like we're a group, we feel like we're a single person, because we really are. And your advertisements should portray that. Develop a relationship with your imaginary friend. The more you get to know your imaginary friends, the more you get to know your marketplace. The more you get to know your marketplace, the easier it is to speak to them through all of the advertisements you put out.

HERE ARE MY BIGGEST TAKEAWAYS

One, become your audience. Watch what they watch, read what they read, go where they go. Two, get into the mind of your ideal prospect. Enter the conversation. Three, focus your advertising on your market. Focus the benefit-driven message that your customer wants. Not you but what your customer wants. Four, the biggest takeaway is talk to your imaginary friend—because best friends share secrets.

I think that's all I've got. I hope you were taking notes, because the most important part of your business is finding out what your customers actually want. It doesn't matter whether you're doing terrible in your marketing efforts or if you think you're doing well, applying these techniques will skyrocket your conversions.

Evolution of Consciousness for the Entrepreneur

Accelerate Your Consciousness, Master Your Life

AUDREE TARA WEITZMAN

"Be the change that you wish to see in the world."

– Mahatma Gandhi

"With great power comes great responsibility"

– Voltaire, Uncle Ben Spiderman

We have been through the Industrial Evolution, the Scientific Evolution and the Technological Evolution. Now is the time for the Evolution of Consciousness. A term prevalent in the personal growth and transformational communities, the Evolution of Consciousness comes out of the ever growing New Age movement. It involves the process of self-awareness and the awakening of the human mind. In truth, it is about personally understanding and awakening to our own behaviors, belief systems and the answers to two critical questions: "Does this serve me?" and "Do I want to live this way?

What does this have to do with you, the entrepreneur? Self-awareness can be a powerful tool in the development of your success.

YOUR THOUGHTS AND BEHAVIORS CREATE YOUR REALITY

We are facing a critical time in our human history. I say critical because our economy, ecology and the human race are struggling for survival. The stress of maintaining your life and excelling to a better way of living has become unbalanced in the "me" culture that we have become. This struggle for survival has an effect on a personal scale: financial hardships, loss of jobs, market crashes, housing devaluations and a lack of well being. We are living fearful lives and have lost connections to both our inner selves and the outer world around us.

You can say that this cataclysmic way of thinking has gone on for centuries. Why do we now need to become aware of our behaviors and how we live? It is because all that we have accomplished, created and discovered can now be utilized for the self-preservation of the planet and the human race. We can take what we have learned and create a way of life that supports community, growth, prosperity and the regeneration of a damaged ecology. I see the Evolution of Consciousness as a coming together of all the past evolutionary processes, and the using of our higher awareness to shift and change the way we live in the world. We can then create a world where we are living to our fullest potential.

So, how does an entrepreneur fit into this world of instability and chaos? Every entrepreneur is a visionary. You think outside the box. Your thoughts and belief systems control who you are and what you become. You are looking for a way to succeed beyond what is expected of you. At the same time, however, everyone else in your life has his or her limited thoughts and belief systems. The outside support for your great adventure (owning your own business) is, therefore, weak, or sometimes non-existent. The evolution of your consciousness and the awareness of your mind's thoughts and belief systems will be your strongest supporter on the road to success.

Human beings are automatically hardwired for failure. It is ingrained in our being that we are less than perfect. Most people live their lives with minds full of negative thoughts. Those thoughts keep telling them they are not good enough, or that they do not have the power to create an amazing life. In fact, those thoughts often say "you do not deserve to have an amazing life". On average, people walk through life sick, poor and lacking enthusiasm or joy for life. They go to school, and then work at a job that meets less than their fullest potential.

You are the exception. For you, there is one big difference in life; you have a dream to do something different. You want to make a difference or do something better than anyone else does. How are you going to accomplish your dreams and live to your fullest potential with all the obstacles knocking at your door? The secret is to evolve your consciousness.

Consciousness by definition means to be aware or have self- awareness. To evolve your consciousness is to follow a process that leads to an unfolding of your self-awareness — that is, the awareness of how you live and behave according to your thoughts and belief systems. And, the evolved consciousness of an entrepreneur is a mindset that allows you to transform yourself continuously into the most successful you. You can then live your life purpose, be in a state of well being and accomplish your heart's desire.

Imagine what it will be like when you are acting and living in your highest potential. Your business, branding, marketing, the operations of your company and your relationships —with yourself, your partners and employees, your audience and clients — will all flow in an effortless way. Imagine your life flowing in abundance, with the ability to see your visions clearly and to manifest your dreams into reality. That is what the evolution of your consciousness will do for you. That is why your Evolution of Consciousness is the most important piece of the puzzle, your greatest tool for success.

THE PROCESS OF AN EVOLVED CONSCIOUSNESS

So how do you become this evolved conscious mastermind of business and personal success? How do you evolve into your fullest potential? There is a guided process to give you the tools you need to clear out the old patterning and create an awakening. The steps are:

1. Acquiring the knowledge or belief that everything is energy.

The first step involves understanding and adopting the belief that you are made up of energy. Actually, everything is energy — a vibrational frequency of wave-like patterns that make up our universe. Energy is an electromagnetic charge that is within and surrounds your body Material objects are slow moving vibrational frequencies (energy) that make up matter. Thoughts are fast moving vibrational frequencies that are invisible to the naked eye, but still move and create our reality. This concept is sometimes abstract, but there is a lot of information to research at your leisure. You may want to read about The Law of Attraction or about manifesting your visions into reality. You might also watch the movie "The Secret".

As an entrepreneur, your greatest tool will be your knowledge of energy and how to manage it to master your life, your relationships and your business. Energy affects how we are in relationship to ourselves and others. It impacts how we feel on a daily basis and how our vision of life's purpose or our business is projected and manifested into the world.

For example, there are some people who, for no reason, you just cannot seem to like. They are very negative, and you feel drained when you see them. Then, there are other people who you love to be around because they are happy, have a glow about them and are especially positive. You might say it's about how they act or behave, but it is really about the energy that they put out into the world. The same goes for your business. If you know about energy you can shift the energies in your life to attract the clients you want.

Importantly, your energy moves based on your thought process. That is why they say if you have negative thoughts you will get sick. This is true. Your thoughts create energy. In an instant, you can shift your negative thoughts to positive ones. And in turn you can change your negative energy into positive energy. In sum, "*Energy goes where consciousness flows*".

Energy is an inherent tool at your disposal; a tool that, if you choose not to use, will be there anyway, reacting to your subconscious mind, an event, which you do not want to happen in your life.

2. Grounding your energy so that you become a stable force of energy.

Life is chaos. Constantly shifting, moving and changing. There is no way to predict or control what happens in your life. This is the cause of all stress, anxiety and grief. I see life, especially during times of transformation, as a tornado swirling around you. It becomes very difficult to deal with things or to make the proper decisions (or even function, for that matter) when life is coming at you like a storm. The drama of life picks you up and lands you in any place, usually on the top of your head. And, for an entrepreneur, this tornado takes on speed and velocity, tenfold. Flying by the seat of your pants is an understatement.

If you are not careful, the decision-making process can mean life or death for your business, your dreams, your life purpose and your financial stability. Grounding your energy will allow you to be calm and stable while the chaos of life is swirling about you. You can become the calm in the center of the storm. In this calm place, you are able to see the whole picture of what is in front of you, and you will no longer be held hostage by emotional reactions to any drama. There is a centered feeling within you, and that is when you will be most effective.

In my training as a healer, I have found that grounding meditation is the foundation for any energy/healing work. You cannot be effective at moving energy if you are not grounded. You cannot make important life altering or business altering decisions if you are not grounded.

To make stable calm decisions, your energy needs to be in your body. I know that sounds a bit strange but, as humans, we have the habit of moving our energies up and outside of our physical bodies. We are not even aware of what we are doing. The energy leaves the physical body because of the emotional pain and suffering that we experience from life; it is easier to cope when we do not feel the pain.

When the energetic body is not connected to the physical form, it causes the body to feel anxious. It can cause a sense of being out of control, unsafe. This experience may cause physical symptoms like heart palpitations and other unproductive side effects. Think about a balloon on a string that is not connected to anything else. The balloon floats away. That is your energy and your consciousness floating away and, with it, the ability to function effectively.

Actually, it is extremely important to ground your energy into the earth itself. Some people have done yoga or used other techniques, such as guided meditation, and imagined roots growing from their feet into the ground. These techniques are based on centuries old teachings that say to anchor your body energy into the earth about three to four feet. There is real science behind these practices. There are electromagnetic grids in the earth's surface, and we connect the energy body into the earth's electromagnetic grids. This gives us a sense of security, belonging and calm.

In 2004, while doing my grounding techniques for meditation and healing work, I discovered a relatively new technique. I was forced to go deeper into the earth to ground my energy. I felt the connection of my energy field anchoring into something very powerful. What I have since learned is that I was anchoring into a permanent electromagnetic field of the earth. Although there is no science as of yet to validate what I was doing, through time and experience I have found this to be a very powerful grounding technique. I have taught it to many of my clients, some with stage four cancers, some facing terminal illnesses (they are in various places of instability).

I also have used this technique with my clients going through life transitions and major upheavals, as well as with those needing to feel safe and calm before making important life decisions. My clients who have used this grounding technique instantaneously felt an improved state of being. There is no waiting; the improved state of being happens as soon as you do the technique.

And, with practice, this technique becomes so easy that it is requires just a quick thought to become grounded; your consciousness and your physical body are calm, centered and balanced in a way that makes you feel safe and unaffected by what is happening around you. You will then begin to live and function through non-emotional reactions to the chaos and drama of life. This will be a great tool in your daily functioning. And, it can determine your success rate in making important business and life decisions.

To learn about this technique and how to use it on your own, please visit www.agilitrix.com.

3. Using energy to clear your negative thoughts and belief systems.

The entrepreneur is a master visionary. The spark of his or her thoughts and the dreams that they build, lead to the creation of a product or business, to fill the needs of the many. Entrepreneurs go against society's grain and the protests of the subconscious mind. Then there is the ego; everyone is watching you, secretly wanting you to fail. Or your own self-sabotage tries to take you down — not to mention how nerve-wracking it can be to make all the correct decisions about branding and marketing yourself and your business.

As an entrepreneur, your mindset must be clear and clean of any negative thoughts. Since thoughts are energy, they can literally reach out and affect your relationship with the outside world. It is, therefore, imperative that you erase any negative thoughts from your mind. Being successful is based on how well you manage and clear your thoughts, your consciousness and your energy.

So, what are negative thoughts? They are the ones that speak to you in your mind and judge everything that you do. Sometimes they are things your parents have told you, or they are based on experiences you had in the past. Some thoughts are from you, telling yourself you are not worthy, good enough, smart enough, do not have any money; the list goes on.

Then there are thoughts of your own greatness, how amazing you are and how no one can beat you or your product. Those thoughts will get you in trouble too; in business a thought can keep you from paying attention to improving your products or services.

In sum, thoughts are your ego, and your ego is a manifestation of an untruth. It is how you perceive yourself and the world based on past experiences. The ego makes up stories for us to believe and cuts us off from having an experience based in the present moment. It is the ego that will destroy your hopes and dreams. This is not ego bashing; the ego has long served you and has been a great asset in so many ways. But it has been running the "show" for your whole life. Now, to reach your fullest potential and the best life or business you can create, your ego needs to take a step back. At **agilitrix.com,** I give you a tool to clear your negative mind set gracefully, quickly and easily.

The process of the Evolution of Consciousness is the empowerment of you taking responsibility for your life. You become the master of your reality and create the life or business that you desire. When you are aware of your negative thoughts and behavior patterns, and you make the decision to let them go, you move into a place of positive thoughts, and begin to manifest a very powerful reality for yourself. This reality is filled with a presence of your own truth, living in the moment and knowing that you have the ability and tools to have what you desire.

4. Manifesting your desires from the heart.

The concept of manifesting your desires (or creating your reality) is something that has been much talked about in the past few years. When the movie, "The Secret," came out, it introduced the idea that it is possible to have the life you desire by asking for it. In fact, "The Secret" became the most popular source of information on manifesting and The Law of Attraction. What the movie doesn't mention is that this information about manifesting your desire, is based in an old paradigm (knowledge) used in a time when the earth vibrated at a different energetic frequency. There is a science to it, which you can read about in detail in my book, *Body Of Light, the Evolution of Consciousness Through the New Chakra System.*

The crucial point coming out of that science is that something about The Law of Attraction has changed and, so, the technique for manifesting has changed. Now, energy is very fast moving, and that changes the way we relate to ourselves and each other. We are coming into the world of peace; we are shifting into an era of living in our hearts. Why is that important for manifestation?

The old way to manifest was to have a vision which would shift your thoughts and move the energy to create your desires. Easy, right? It works, but is problematic in that, often, along with the thought of what you wanted, came a thought of how it might be impossible or that you are unworthy, In that case, the negative thought canceled out the vision.

The solution in this new energy is not to have a vision. Instead, go deeper, out of your mind (where the vision is) and into your heart, where your desire is. Yes, the heart is where manifestation takes place in this new era! For a great tool to teach you how to manifest from the heart and experience manifestation in this higher vibrational energy, please go to **(agilitrix.com).**

To create and manifest what you desire into reality, it must be done from the heart. There can be no attachment to how it manifests. There is no business plan for manifestation. That is not The Law of Attraction. The Law of Attraction says like energies (thoughts move energy) attract to each other and what you desire will manifest. The most powerful energetic wave patterns are in the heart.

"... the heart is far more than a simple pump ... (it is) a highly complex, self-organized information processing center with its own functional "brain" that communicates with and influences the cranial brain... These influences profoundly affect brain function and most of the body's major organs, and ultimately determine the quality of life." — **The Institute of HeartMath**

If you are going into business to create destruction or greed, the techniques I've been talking about are not for you; it won't work. Those negative emotions are low vibrational frequencies and thought forms and will no longer be tolerated in this new paradigm. However, If you are envisioning a business product or service to help make the world a better place because you know that you can improve on a system, or want to make a difference in the world and in your life, then this knowledge will work. These tools can only be used for the highest good of man.

Remember that the mind is not a perfected state of being where there are no negative thoughts. You must drop all of your vision into your heart. Breathe in your business plan — not the step-by-step process, but the end result of your goals and vision. Feel what it is like to have your successful business, all the support that you need and beyond what you can imagine. Expect that you will have the life of your dreams, feel what it's like to live in that place of complete happiness and then let it go. When negative thoughts come into your mind, use the tools I gave you to release them.

5. Stepping into the new paradigm of business and living your highest potential.

Once you have learned this process of understanding and harnessing your body energies for good, you will be able to create and manifest the business of your dreams — no, more than that — a business beyond your wildest dreams. This is especially true for entrepreneurs because coming from an evolved consciousness means that you will:

- Maintain calm and balance to make important decisions

- Clear your limiting negative thoughts and belief systems

- Living your fullest potential, vibrant and healthy — physically mentally emotional and spiritually

- Be able to manifest your desires quickly and easily

Nothing in your business, or your life, will ever be the same.

Audree Weitzman uses her knowledge and skill as a healer, reads the Akashic Records and incorporates her training in energy based life coaching into a formula she developed called Intuitive Strategies Coaching, please go to www.agilitrix.com for more information.

www.ingramcontent.com/pod-product-compliance
Lightning Source LLC
Chambersburg PA
CBHW060556200326
41521CB00007B/590